The Political Philosophy of
Merleau-Ponty

PHILOSOPHY NOW

GENERAL EDITOR: Roy Edgley, Professor of Philosophy, University of Sussex.

Professor Edgley writes: 'English-speaking philosophy since the Second World War has been dominated by the method of linguistic analysis, the latest phase of the analytical movement in the early years of the century.

That method is defined by certain doctrines about the nature and scope both of philosophy and of the other subjects from which it distinguishes itself; and those doctrines reflect the fact that in this period philosophy and other intellectual activities have been increasingly monopolised by the universities, social institutions with a special role. Though expansive in number of practitioners, these activities have cultivated an expertise that in characteristic ways has narrowed their field of vision. As our twentieth-century world has staggered from crisis to crisis, English-speaking philosophy in particular has submissively dwindled into a humble academic specialism, on its own understanding isolated from substantive issues in other disciplines, from the practical problems facing society, and from contemporary Continental thought.

The books in this series are united by nothing except discontent with this state of affairs. Convinced that the analytical movement has spent its momentum, its latest phase no doubt its last, the series seeks in one way or another to push philosophy out of its ivory tower.'

1. FREEDOM AND LIBERATION   Benjamin Gibbs
2. HEGEL'S PHENOMENOLOGY: A PHILOSOPHICAL INTRODUCTION   Richard Norman
3. ART, AN ENEMY OF THE PEOPLE   Roger Taylor
4. PHILOSOPHY AND ITS PAST   Jonathan Rée, Michael Ayers and Adam Westoby
5. RULING ILLUSIONS: PHILOSOPHY AND THE SOCIAL ORDER   Anthony Skillen
6. THE WORK OF SARTRE: VOLUME 1: SEARCH FOR FREEDOM   István Mészáros
7. THE WORK OF SARTRE: VOLUME 2: THE CHALLENGE OF HISTORY   István Mészáros
8. THE POSSIBILITY OF NATURALISM   Roy Bhaskar
9. THE REAL WORLD OF IDEOLOGY   Joe McCarney
10. HEGEL, MARX AND DIALECTIC: A DEBATE   Richard Norman and Sean Sayers
11. THE DIALECTIC OF REVOLUTION   Chris Arthur
12. SCIENCE AND IDEOLOGY   Roy Edgley
13. THE POLITICAL PHILOSOPHY OF MERLEAU-PONTY   Sonia Kruks
14. PHILOSOPHICAL IDEOLOGIES   Roy Bhaskar

The Political Philosophy of Merleau-Ponty

SONIA KRUKS
*Honorary Fellow in Political Science,
University of Wisconsin – Madison*

THE HARVESTER PRESS · SUSSEX
HUMANITIES PRESS · NEW JERSEY

First published in Great Britain in 1981 by
THE HARVESTER PRESS LIMITED
Publisher: John Spiers
16 Ship Street, Brighton, Sussex

and in the USA by
HUMANITIES PRESS INC.,
Atlantic Highlands, New Jersey 07716

© Sonia Kruks, 1981

British Library Cataloguing in Publication Data
Kruks, Sonia
  The political philosophy of Merleau Ponty. — (Philosophy now).
  1. Merleau-Ponty, Maurice — Political science
  2. Political science
  I. Title
  320'.01   JC261.M47
  ISBN 0-85527-846-3
  ISBN 0-85527-428-x Pbk

Humanities Press Inc.
ISBN 0-391-02226-1

Photoset in Great Britain by
Rowland Phototypesetting Limited
Bury St Edmunds, Suffolk
and printed by
Redwood Burn Ltd, Trowbridge and Esher

All rights reserved

This book is dedicated to my parents
Leo and Sima Kruks

Contents

Acknowledgements ix

Abbreviations x

Introduction xi

PART 1: FOUNDATIONS

1. The 'philosophy of existence'   3
   The critique of idealism and positivism
   The body-subject and the natural world
   The social world
   Freedom and history

2. Merleau-Ponty, Hegel and the dialectic   24
   Merleau-Ponty's interpretations of Hegel
   Critique of the Hegelian dialectic
   Merleau-Ponty's dialectic

PART 2: TOWARDS MARXISM

3. Marxism and the 'philosophy of existence'   45
   The materialist method
   Meaning in history
   'Praxis'
   Critique of Merleau-Ponty's Marxism

4. The critique of liberalism   61
   Liberal philosophy
   Liberal ideology
   Some comments on Merleau-Ponty's critique

5. Truth, morality and violence in politics   76
   The possibility of moral action
   The unique role of the proletariat
   Morality, violence and the individual
   Morality, violence and the proletarian movement

Contents

PART 3: RETREAT

6. The rejection of Marxist politics — 101
   The 'conversion'
   The failure of Marxist theory
   The dialectic in action
   Sartre's subjectivism

7. After Marxism — 119
   The 'conversion' and philosophy
   The universal in politics
   Political activity and inactivity
   Marxism as the disclosure of Being

Concluding Remarks — 133

Chronology — 138

Bibliography One — 143

Bibliography Two — 145

Index — 151

Acknowledgements

TO BEGIN at the beginning, I would like to thank Ralph Miliband for encouraging me to make a study of Merleau-Ponty's political philosophy and John Charvet, my supervisor at the London School of Economics, for enabling and encouraging me to continue it. For reading and commenting on earlier drafts of material in Part 1, I would like to thank Paul Hirst, Hide Ishiguro and Joan Safran. For their general support and for helpful comments on material in Chapter 3, I would like to thank former colleagues at the City of London Polytechnic, in particular, Jerry Palmer and Rene Saran. For a critical reading and discussion of an earlier version of the whole work, thanks go to Ernest Gellner and Anthony Manser. With David Archard I had some interesting discussions on Merleau-Ponty's relationship to Sartre and with Roy Carr-Hill on the political and intellectual background to Merleau-Ponty's work, for which thanks to both of them. Finally, I would like to thank Ben Wisner for his many suggestions, and continual encouragement while this book was being written.

I acknowledge the publisher's permission to quote from *Humanism and Terror* by Maurice Merleau-Ponty, copyright © by Beacon Press. Reprinted by permission of Beacon Press.

List of Abbreviations

The following abbreviations are used to designate those works of Merleau-Ponty which are most widely cited. Dates given below in brackets refer to the date of the original French publication, while the titles given are those of the English translations, to which I refer throughout.

AD	Adventures of the Dialectic, 1974 (1955)
HT	Humanism and Terror, 1969 (1947)
PP	Phenomenology of Perception, 1962 (1945)
Pri Per	The Primacy of Perception, 1964 (1947)
Pr Phil	In Praise of Philosophy, 1963 (1953)
S	Signs, 1964 (1960)
SB	The Structure of Behaviour, 1965 (1942)
SNS	Sense and Non-Sense, 1964 (1948)
TL	Themes from the Lectures, 1970 (1968, posthumous)
VI	The Visible and the Invisible, 1968 (1964, posthumous)

Introduction

WHEN Merleau-Ponty's major work, the *Phenomenology of Perception*, was published in 1945, it received only one short review in Britain, a review that dismissed it as 'failing to be a genuine contribution to philosophy' (Anon, 1946). Since that time the work of Merleau-Ponty has become better known and respected in Britain, but his reputation is still overshadowed by that of his former friend and collaborator, Jean-Paul Sartre.

Born within three years of each other, both as Sartre has said, of petit-bourgeois republican families (1965, p. 159), they both studied philosophy in Paris in the inter-war years and, independently of each other, moved towards phenomenology as an alternative to the inward-looking French academic philosophy of the time. Their paths first crossed significantly however only in German occupied France, in 1941, when they belonged to the same short-lived intellectuals' Resistance group, 'Socialism and Liberty'. Thereafter, they met more often, discussed phenomenology and, from 1943 onwards, talked of founding a journal together.

In October 1945 that journal was born: *Les Temps Modernes*, symbol of 'existentialism' in the heady years following the Liberation and associated in the public mind above all with the name of Sartre. Novelist, playwright, speaker, as well as philosopher, Sartre became a cult figure, both adored and vilified, but continually in the limelight in that period. But as he was later to make clear (1965, p. 171), the dramatics of Left Bank 'existentialism' apart, *Les Temps Modernes* was conceived as a serious political undertaking and it was above all Merleau-Ponty, the somewhat withdrawn teacher of philosophy, who directed that undertaking. In spite of repeated requests from Sartre, Merleau-Ponty refused to have his name on the cover as joint director of the journal. Yet as its political editor, between 1945 and 1950, it was, Sartre insists, Merleau-Ponty and not himself who made the journal an instrument of independent Left analysis and critique.

As both Merleau-Ponty and Sartre saw it, the task of the journal was to be at once committed and detached—committed to socialist solutions to the world's problems, but above all committed to an honest and open scrutiny of the world, to debunking myths and exposing lies, whether of the Right or the Left, as the best way of assisting the development of such solutions. Hence, therefore, the need for detachment, especially in relation to the French Communist Party (PCF) which claimed to be the guardian of left-wing Truth. Following the Liberation, a coalition government was established and the PCF agreed to enter it. The journal was quick to denounce the hypocrisy and manoeuvrings which soon resulted. As information became available, in the late 1940s and early 1950s, on the horrors of Stalinist Russia this was also reported and discussed. Simultaneously however, the journal was attacking both French and international capitalism, for example the beginning of Marshall Aid (see the editorial, July 1948), or American manoeuvring in Greece (Dzelepy, 1949). In 1945 independence movements emerged in many parts of the French Empire, only to be met by heavy repression from the French government. The response to successes of the Vietnamese independence movement was the bombing of Haiphong in November 1946 and the editorial which *Les Temps Modernes* carried in December marked the establishment of a militant anti-colonial policy—a policy which the journal still maintains today.

This book is not, however, about the history of *Les Temps Modernes*.[1] Nor is it about the history of Merleau-Ponty's relationship with Sartre. It is a book about Merleau-Ponty's philosophy, in particular about his political philosophy. Most of the book is concerned with the period up to 1945 during which Merleau-Ponty developed his general philosophical position, his own brand of what has been called 'existential phenomenology' (Part 1), and with the political ideas he developed between 1945 and the early 1950s (Part 2). These ideas were formulated mainly in articles published in *Les Temps Modernes*, many of which were also afterwards published in the two collections, *Humanism and Terror* and *Sense and Non-Sense*. However, although *Les Temps Modernes* provided the main vehicle, the ideas Merleau-Ponty expressed there on politics cannot be understood if we read *only* what appeared in the journal: what I wish to demonstrate above all in this book is the inseparability of Merleau-Ponty's *general* philosophical position and his political philosophy. This is also to say that it is essential not to confuse Merleau-Ponty's political ideas with those of Sartre, even though the two men endorsed each others' writings in the journal, until the early 1950s. Merleau-Ponty's general philosophy might share with Sartre's the labels of 'phenomenological' and 'existential', but there are also fundamental divergences and these extend necessarily to the political philosophies of the two. I do not intend to dwell at length on these divergences, but some of them will become apparent in the course of my account.

I have said that most of the book is concerned with the period prior to the early 1950s. This is, in my opinion, the period of Merleau-Ponty's most interesting and important work. It is the period in which he developed and then used his existential phenomenology to scrutinise the Marxism of his time and to raise what are still today very real questions; questions such as how to avoid reductionist or mechanistic ways of explaining the relationships between the 'economic' and the 'super-structural' elements of a society, or the question of how far revolutionary movements can use violent means without becoming distorted by them. On the whole Merleau-Ponty does not provide clear and definitive answers to the questions he raises. Perhaps it would be true to say that one of the most important lessons he tries to teach us is *not* to expect such answers in politics: there are no cook-books for transforming society, least of all Marxist ones.

Merleau-Ponty died suddenly in 1961. By then he had disagreed with Sartre and resigned from *Les Temps Modernes* (1952), broken openly with Marxism (1955) and withdrawn in pessimism from any position of political commitment. But many of the questions posed in his earlier writings were to surface again in varying forms in the challenging of orthodox Marxism in France in May 1968. This is not to say that one can trace a direct line of influence from Merleau-Ponty's work to the action of the later generation—the development of political ideas is never so simple—but that his writings contributed to the critique of orthodox Marxism out of which the political style of May 1968 at least in part emerged.

Merleau-Ponty's break with Marxism, his unsuccessful search for alternatives and final retreat from political commitment are treated fairly briefly in the last part of the book. As will be apparent, I think Merleau-Ponty's critique of Marxism was extremely weak and that it reveals in fact not only the abandonment of Marxism but also the abandonment of the phenomenological method of the earlier period. What is interesting is that, once again, the political philosophy is inseparable from the general philosophy. Merleau-Ponty's changing political philosophy is of course partly a response to the changing political situation around him. But it has also to be viewed in the context of the gradual—but not explicit—abandonment of his existential phenomenology for a kind of metaphysics in the period between 1952 and 1961. The fact that Merleau-Ponty ended up in metaphysics and political withdrawal does not however detract from the importance of his earlier work. Paradoxically, the weaknesses of his last political writings serve to underscore the strength and pertinence of his earlier political philosophy.

Notes

1 For a book which does give this history, see Burnier (1966), and also the appropriate volumes of Simone de Beauvoir's autobiography (1963, 1965).

PART 1:

FOUNDATIONS

1 The 'Philosophy of Existence'

Merleau-Ponty said towards the end of his life that he had always wanted to study philosophy (Chapsal, 1960, p. 148). In 1927, aged nineteen, he entered the Ecole Normale in Paris to read philosophy. While what he encountered there did not succeed in killing his passion, it appears to have left him profoundly dissatisfied. The dominant philosophies were all thoroughly idealist (the Neo-Kantianism of Brunschvicg, the 'Spiritualism' of Lavelle and Le Senne, the Thomism of Gilson), and there was a great emphasis on individualist ethics. Individual consciousness and individual conscience were, one could say, the two main themes of French philosophy.[1] Already anachronistic after World War One, this kind of philosophy became increasingly so as the 1930s progressed, in the face of acute economic depression and the rise of Fascism. Insulated from such uncomfortable realities by its continued focus on the inner life of the private individual, French academic philosophy became increasingly unable to say anything about the world around it.

Like other young people with whom he was later to be associated, including Sartre and Simone de Beauvoir, Merleau-Ponty began, in the mid-1930s, when a doctoral candidate, to search for alternatives. This search was not random. It was clearly motivated by two interconnected desires. Firstly, the desire to reject the idealist postulates which underlay the current philosophy, but to do so without returning to what Merleau-Ponty believed to be the equally erroneous classical alternative, positivism. Secondly, Merleau-Ponty wished, through his rejection of idealism, to make philosophy more relevant, in the sense of giving it a function in explaining everyday life. Philosophy should not stay encapsulated within its own constructed world; it needed to be able to grasp the world around it and communicate with that world.

The alternatives which Merleau-Ponty sought and was to

synthesise were already on the horizon in the 1930s. As he himself would have been the first to admit, no new philosophy ever starts from a 'tabula rasa', but from an atmosphere of ideas already existing. The idea that philosophy should be the study of the 'concrete', or of 'lived' human existence, was already gaining ground in France, in the work of Wahl (1932), Minkowski (1933) and, above all, Marcel (1935), who can perhaps be described as the father of French 'existentialism', although his starting point was religious while that of later thinkers was not. From Germany other new ideas, those of phenomenology, were beginning to spread slowly to France, arguing that the task of philosophy should be above all revelation and description—the 'return to things themselves', as both Husserl and Heidegger called it. Husserl, usually regarded as the founder of modern phenomenology, gave a series of lectures in Paris in 1929 which it is probable that Merleau-Ponty attended. Another growing German movement which Merleau-Ponty was to draw on came not from philosophy but from psychology, the *Gestalt* school, based in Frankfurt. This school focussed primarily on the question of explaining perception, but did so in a way which suggested a possible way of resolving the philosophical dualism embodied in the debate between idealism and positivism. The rediscovery of Hegel in France was also of great importance for Merleau-Ponty. The study of Hegel had virtually not existed in the French universities (Koyré, 1931) until Kojève began his famous series of lectures in 1933. In the concept of dialectic Merleau-Ponty was to find yet another essential element of his own philosophy.

The Critique of Idealism and Positivism

It would be true to say that Merleau-Ponty's own philosophy, a philosophy which he insisted was neither idealist nor positivist but a 'philosophy of existence', was already formulated in its essentials by 1938. That was the year in which he completed the manuscript of his first book, *The*

Structure of Behaviour. It was, however, greatly broadened and deepened by the time he published what is undoubtedly his major work, the *Phenomenology of Perception*, in 1945. In *The Structure of Behaviour* Merleau-Ponty remains primarily in the field of clinical psychology in discussing kinds of explanation of animal and human behaviour. In the *Phenomenology of Perception*, Merleau-Ponty situates himself much more explicitly within phenomenological philosophy and goes beyond the questions of perception and behaviour to treat such 'classical' themes of philosophy as time, space knowing (the 'Cogito') and human freedom within his own philosophical framework.

Both *The Structure of Behaviour* and the *Phenomenology of Perception* proceed through a process of critique of existing theories towards their synthesis in a new theory. *The Structure of Behaviour* begins with a critique of the kind of explanation of behaviour which Merleau-Ponty calls variously positivism, scientism, empiricism. This way of explaining reduces man to an 'object' whose behaviour is the outcome of external causes or stimuli. Its approach is atomistic and deterministic, allowing for neither the *integrated* nature of behaviour nor the intiating and creative role of consciousness in forming behaviour. Pavlov's theory of conditioning (1964) is critically discussed as a major example of this kind of explanation.

As man is an integrated being we cannot simply partition off different levels of human activity: we cannot make clearcut distinctions between instincts, reflexes and conscious activity. 'Man is not a rational animal. The appearance of reason and mind does not leave intact a sphere of selfenclosed instincts in man' (SB 181). Behaviourist psychology tries to explain human learning in terms of stimulus and response, seeing rewards as the stimuli for learning. But, says Merleau-Ponty, this must mean that learning is a chance process, for the child must accidentally perform correctly before he is rewarded and therefore 'learns' the behaviour. Learning in Merleau-Ponty's view is not such a chance activity, for it does not consist in acquiring a capacity to repeat an action mechanically, but consists in learning the appropriate but *differing* responses required by situations; learning involves adaptation to situations and must presuppose what Merleau-Ponty calls an *intentional* interaction with the environment.

At the other end of the spectrum from behaviourism, idealist, or what Merleau-Ponty calls 'critical' or 'intellectualist' approaches, are also unable adequately to describe behaviour, since they divorce man from the world and from his own body in asserting the priority of consciousness over matter. Descartes' 'cogito', for example, might reveal a world—but it is a world of *thoughts* only. For Descartes and his successors (including Kant), the priority of mind not only locks man in a world of pure consciousness, of purely intellectual knowing, it also reduces the world to an object of consciousness, postulating a dualism of subject and object which Merleau-Ponty does not accept.

If, for Merleau-Ponty, man is neither a causally determined 'thing', nor an undetermined consciousness, we must ask: what are the main characteristics of his being? What is the basis of his behaviour?

Merleau-Ponty starts to work towards his own answer to these questions mainly on the basis of Gestalt psychology, which he interprets in an existential and dialectical manner. Gestalt psychology (for example, Koffka, 1925, Koehler, 1930, Goldstein, 1934), had demonstrated experimentally that perception involves an interactive process between the perceiver and the perceived in which the perceiver organises his perceptions to form a coherent 'gestalt' or 'form' or 'structure'. Merleau-Ponty raises this experimental observation to a general proposition of existential philosophy: in the concept of 'structure' we can capture the meeting point of 'existence' and consciousness and show that they are interdependent, neither the 'cause' of the other (SB 206–7), and thus transcend the dualism inherent in both positivist and idealist philosophies.

Merleau-Ponty describes the process of emergence of structures as a 'dialectic'. There is a 'circular process such as does not exist in the physical world, through which the individual organism . . . itself measures the action of things upon itself and itself delimits its milieu' (SB 148). This dialectical relationship, 'brings about the appearance of new relations' (SB 148). It engages the organism in a work of transformation of its environment and thus necessitates the emergence of yet further new 'structures'. To describe behaviour—animal or human—adequately is to elucidate the genesis and meaning of 'structures' or, says Merleau-Ponty, to describe the 'intentionality' of the world.

Although the concept of 'intentionality' is introduced in *The Structure of Behaviour* (p. 224), it is only fully developed in *The Phenomenology of Perception*. A key concept in Husserl's phenomenology, its centrality in *The Phenomenology of Perception* is an indication of Merleau-Ponty's more explicit identification of his own philosophy with Husserlian phenomenology by 1945. *The Phenomenology of Perception* is not only a work of the 'philosophy of existence', it is also a work of 'existential phenomenology'—that is, it uses phenomenology as its means of studying existence. As Ricoeur has put it: '. . . phenomenology becomes a method and is placed in the service of a dominating problem-set, viz, the problems concerning existence' (1967, p. 203). This is not to say that phenomenology is *only* a method, a technique, but that its philosophical presuppositions permit the development of a method particularly appropriate for the study of existence.

The question of Merleau-Ponty's relationship with Husserl is complex and can certainly not be discussed in detail here. Merleau-Ponty might have been a disciple of Husserl, but he was not a very faithful one. The question is further complicated by the fact that Husserl's own thought underwent profound modifications throughout his life.

A mathematician by training, Husserl set out initially on a search for the 'foundations' of mathematical knowledge, a search which was to lead him to the pursuit of an indubitable basis for logic and from thence to the wider question, earlier formulated by Descartes: do we have any knowledge of which we can be certain? Husserl's searches led him to conclude that the only way to certain or 'apoditic' knowledge was on a circuitous route via the subjective, through the study of the process in which phenomena appear for our consciousness. Phenomenology, the method Husserl developed, attempts to study phenomena as they appear for consciousness, refusing to concern itself with the question of whether what exists for consciousness has a reality outside it. But Husserl believed that by studying the phenomenal—

which to start with is all we can be sure exists—it would in fact be possible to arrive at the certain and general foundations of knowledge and to discover the 'essential core' of any phenomenon.

The method for studying and penetrating to the 'essential core' of the phenomenon and arriving at the certain foundations of knowledge, Husserl called the 'reduction', or the 'bracketing' process. This is the process of systematically ignoring or suspending the 'real world', as we assume our everyday world to be, in order to reveal the phenomenal world, the world as it appears for consciousness. In the *Cartesian Meditations* (1961; the original lectures were given in 1929), Husserl argues that the process of bracketing finally reveals to us the 'transcendental ego', a general constituting consciousness which 'intends' the world, as the basis of knowledge. In the last analysis it is thus our own consciousness which brings the world into being for us. The concept of the 'transcendental ego' thus implies a thorough going idealism which Merleau-Ponty did not accept, even though he accepted the method of the reduction.

Merleau-Ponty had probably read no works of Husserl's later than the *Cartesian Meditations* when he completed *The Structure of Behaviour*. However, in 1939 he visited the Husserl Archives in Louvain. While there, he read parts of the manuscript of Husserl's last, unpublished work, the *Crisis* (Van Breda, 1962) and it appears to have been on this work that he drew most in developing his own conception of phenomenology. In the *Crisis* Husserl moved away from his earlier idealism, arguing that what is finally revealed as the certain foundation of knowledge through the reduction is not, after all, the 'transcendental ego', but what he called the 'life-world'. The 'life-world' is the 'pre-given', which precedes and supports all operations of thought:

It belongs to what is taken for granted, prior to all scientific thought and all philosophical questioning, that the world is—always is in advance—and that every correction of an opinion, whether an experiential or other opinion, presupposes the already existing world, namely as the horizon of what in the given case is indubitably valid as existing (1970, p. 110).

Merleau-Ponty's interpretation of this concept is perhaps

rather free. On the basis of the *Crisis* he interprets Husserl's late work as not only 'existential', that is, capable of grasping existence without falling into the dualism of either idealism or positivism, but also as 'dialectical', since it necessarily captures the dialectical nature of existence.

The concept of 'intentionality', which I have said is a key concept in Husserl's work (both early and late) and which is also central in Merleau-Ponty's phenomenology, is closely linked with the method of the reduction. Indeed, says Merleau-Ponty, 'it is understandable only through the reduction' (PP xvii). Merleau-Ponty's account of 'intentionality' is connected in particular with Husserl's concept of the 'life-world'. 'Intentionality', as the term is used in phenomenology, is not to be confused with its more common meaning, conscious action towards a pre-defined goal. Perhaps we can best capture the idea negatively: to say that there exists 'intentionality' is to say that the world is essentially *not* chaotic, essentially *not* random. It is to say that it necessarily has a 'structure', or meaning, as we encounter it. 'What distinguishes intentionality . . . is that the unity of the world, before being posited by knowledge in a specific act of identification, is 'lived' as ready-made or already there . . .' (PP xvii). It thus becomes possible to talk about 'intentionality' as a property of things as well as of people, since all things inhere in the meaningful structure of the world: 'to "understand" is to take in the total intention . . . the unique mode of existing expressed in the properties of the pebble, glass or piece of wax, in all the events of a revolution, in all the thoughts of a philosopher' (PP xviii).

The 'intentionality' of things is not, however, wholly independent of us—although their meaning could not be there without us and meaning can only be meaning for us. For meaning is not *only* a product of our consciousness, as classical idealism argues (PP ix). On the contrary, 'The world is there before any possible analysis of mine'. (PP x). What Merleau-Ponty is attempting to express in his concept of 'intentionality' is the meaning that arises from the simultaneous interdependence and autonomy of man and the world. Man is, to use the more Hegelian vocabulary Merleau-Ponty often employs, both an 'object', that is, a physical or material being, and a 'subject', that is, having consciousness, will and the capacity to act *on* the physical world of objects. It is this double-sidedness of human existence, summed up in the idea that man is a 'body-subject',[2] which makes 'meaning', 'structure', 'intention', possible.

The Body-Subject and the Natural World

The concept of the 'body-subject' appears, at first consideration, paradoxical, for the body is normally regarded as an object. Either as the object of external forces in materialist thought, or as the object of consciousness in idealist philosophy. In regarding the body as a subject, Merleau-Ponty is denying both these views and is asserting that it is only through our materiality, through our bodily existence, that we are able to 'know' the world, which is also to create it.

But to 'know' the world through one's body is not to 'know' it in the way pure consciousness does. Bodily 'knowledge' differs in two ways from that of 'a universal constituting consciousness' (PP 147).[3] Firstly, it is 'situated' knowledge. Our body is *in* the world, and thus cannot know the world from a distance, but only from our own time and place. Our knowledge of the world varies as our situation within it alters and there can be no universal or a-temporal, no absolute or objective knowledge.

Secondly, bodily knowledge differs from that of a constituting consciousness in that it is in the first instance 'perceptive' knowledge and not knowledge of reason. Unlike the latter, it does not arise through contemplation but through intentionality when we act. Our fundamental experience is that of our bodies. We come to know the world and to realise our interconnectedness with the world through our bodies, and this knowledge is sensual or perceptive before it is conscious.

The body is the contact point which makes possible the dialectical relation between man and the world, in which each sustains the other. It is because of the primacy of body, rather than mind, in this relationship that our initial knowledge of the world has to be 'perceptive'—i.e. bodily—rather than of the 'cogito'. Merleau-Ponty talks about a 'tacit cogito' (PP 403), a pre-conscious 'knowing' of ourselves and of existence, as the basis of our knowledge. Reason and philosophy—the 'spoken cogito'—are grounded in and sustained by the 'tacit cogito'. Perception always remains experientially prior to reason. The 'tacit cogito', he writes, 'does not constitute the world, it divines the world's presence round about it as a field not provided by itself . . . the tacit cogito, the presence of oneself to onself, is anterior to any philosophy' (PP 404).

But, we might ask, what kind of world can it be that the body 'divines' prior to rational consciousness? Certainly it is not the ordered world of science or philosophy, for such order is elicited by scientific or philosophical activity and does not exist prior to such activity. The world that I 'know' or 'perceive' through my body is variously described by Merleau-Ponty as a 'primordial layer' (PP 219) of being, as 'the mode of the impersonal "One"' (PP 240), and corresponds very roughly to Husserl's notion of the 'life-world'.

It is at the level of the interaction of the body with this inchoate being that the dialectic has its source. Here the dichotomy of man as subject ('for-itself') and world, as object ('in-itself') can be transcended, since the body lives its oneness with the world without a definite line between the two being possible; body and world coincide. It is at the level of preconscious sense experience that man first creates and elicits meaning through his dialectical interaction with the world. All the more conscious and elucidated structures of meaning, including philosophy and the shape of history and politics, therefore arise, in the final analysis, from this preconscious level: 'it is upon our experience of the world that all our logical operations concerned with significance must be based' (PP 328). It is just *because* it arises from the primary dialectic that all conscious experience, including philsophy, is guaranteed as also being of and in the world.

It is also because it arises from this primary dialectic that philosophy can never wholly detach itself from the preconscious or the pre-logical. Its task is not, as current linguistic philosophy suggests, to eliminate the confused or ambiguous in our ways of thinking—and indeed it could never succeed at such a task. The world *is* ambiguous and philosophy necessarily partakes of this worldly quality. 'The task of our century', Merleau-Ponty wrote a couple of years after the *Phenomenology of Perception* was published, is 'the attempt to explore the irrational and integrate it into an expanded reason' (SNS 63). But this integration does not imply the elimination of the irrational.

It is perhaps appropriate to ask at this point how Merleau-Ponty deals with one of the classic problems of philosophy; namely that of truth. If neither materialist nor idealist philosophy is able to provide us with adequate criteria for truth because of their respective one-sidedness, in what way *can* we recognise truth?

Philosophy and all 'logical operations', as we have seen, are rooted in our basic perceptional experience of the world. It is thus at the level of *perception* and not as a question of philosophy that we must first consider the nature of truth. Given that all perception is 'situated' and thus relative, is it in fact possible to talk about 'true' or 'false' perceptions? Merleau-Ponty believes that we *can* make such a distinction, although it cannot be absolute. He discusses the issue in terms of the distinction to be made between valid or 'true' perception and hallucination (PP 334–45).

Since all perception is subjective it cannot be its subjective character that distinguishes hallucination from true perception. But true perception, although subjective, is not *purely* subjective and receives objective confirmation: it opens on to and confirms itself in the world. It is when I *act* on the basis of my perception that I can confirm its truth; or when I share it with others my perception receives an intersubjective confirmation, if it is true. A hallucinatory perception does not have these qualities:

> ... there is no definite path leading from it to all the remaining experiences of the deluded subject, or to the experience of the same. The hallucinatory thing is not, as is the real thing, packed with small perceptions which sustain it in existence. It is an implicit and inarticulate significance (PP 339).

Thus the hallucinatory perception is 'closed', totally subjective and not confirmed by others or in action. However, the confirmation even of our 'true' perceptions can never be absolute, since our perceptions are not *identical* with those of others, nor fully guaranteed in action. Truth and falsity, or error, in perception are not separated absolutely.

The Social World

This far in the exposition, the analysis has been of men as individuals, or of 'man in general'. It has been asked: how is man related to the world? How is the individual 'inserted' into the world so that he is neither a passive 'object' in the order of things, nor a 'subject' who claims to stand outside material existence? I have shown how Merleau-Ponty tries to resolve the subject-object duality through the notion of the body-subject; and how he sees a basic dialectic of the perceiving body and the primordial world supporting conscious life. Through this dialectic man's consciousness and his materiality, his subjectivity and his objectivity are integrated.

But 'man' for Merleau-Ponty is not 'individual man' or 'man in general'; he is man among men. A full description of human existence—the task of phenomenological philosophy and the 'philosophy of existence'—must include also a description of the *human* world, that is, of man's relation to man and of all that grows from it. Human existence is a twofold dialectic. It is as we have seen a dialectic between man and the natural world; but it is also and simultaneously a dialectic *between* man, in which the 'social world' of language, culture and institutions is brought into being. Man's relation to the social world is in many ways a continuation of his relation with the natural world. For the social world is also rooted in the 'One', the pre-conscious level of incipient meanings and is a field within which individuals act, drawing out more explicit meanings and structures from the pre-conscious. Myth, magic, science and legal systems are all, at their different levels, 'crystallisations' of what already exists inchoately in the social world. Similarly, politics can never be conceived as an autonomous area of activity, but can only be fully described if we return to its pre-conscious grounding in the 'One'.

Most of Merleau-Ponty's works after the *Phenomenology* discuss specific aspects of the social world—politics, history, art, literature etc. In these works he generally takes the existence of the social world as 'given': men function within cultures, have institutions and ideas. He examines concrete institutions and ideas without asking how, in general, they are possible. In *The Structure of Behaviour* and *Phenomenology of Perception*, however, he is concerned with this question of how the social world is possible. The question falls into two distinct but connected parts: firstly, how can shared meanings arise, or—in Merleau-Ponty's (and Husserl's) terminology—how is 'intersubjectivity' possible? Secondly, what is the dynamic through which the social world is created? Through what means does it come into existence, endure and change?

The question of intersubjectivity is treated at some length in the final sections of *Phenomenology of Perception*. The discussion would appear to be a reply to Sartre's view of inter-personal relations, as developed in *Being and Nothingness* (1943). Sartre, in Merleau-Ponty's opinion, fails to overcome the duality of subject and object in his philosophy. For if, as with Sartre, the individual is regarded as a subject, a pure consciousness, the world, *including* other people, is for him no more than an object of consciousness. Thus when two people meet each reduces the other to an object, an opaque 'thing-in-itself' which he can observe, but whose perceptions and feelings he cannot share. We have, says Merleau-Ponty, 'the paradox of a consciousness seen from the outside' (PP 349) and intersubjectivity is not possible.

Merleau-Ponty argues that such a view of human relations is mistaken. For man is not a subject in the Sartrean sense, since he is not a subject in the sense of a 'constituting consciousness" (PP 351). Far from the other being a *threat* to my subjectivity, he is an *extension* of it, since his perceptions confirm mine. This is because we are both bodily beings, a composite of objectivity and subjectivity, grounded in the same dialectic with the primordial world (PP 352). Clearly I am not totally transparent to the other person, since I am not so to myself; and clearly our perceptions cannot be identical as we each start from our own unique 'situation', be it spatial or socio-cultural. But because we both, through our bodies, open on to the same natural world and draw our intention from the same source, our perceptions must overlap considerably and we are able to create common areas of meaning, an 'interworld' between us (PP 357).

Thus a world of common meanings, of intersubjectivity, is in principle not only possible but necessary. Meaning, as we have seen, may be pre-conscious, rooted in bodily action. Thus the human 'interworld' may at its simplest level be merely one of bodily significations. But with the use of language, the human 'interworld' grows ever fuller and richer:

> In the experience of dialogue, there is constituted between the other person and myself a common ground; my thought and his are interwoven into a single fabric, my words and those of my interlocutor are called forth by the state of discussion, and they are inserted into a shared operation of which neither of us is the creator (PP 354).

Language, then, outstrips the speaker. Speech is 'an originating realm' (PP 174) in which the meaning of what we say spills out beyond the initial intention of our words. This quality of spilling out beyond itself, of creating an infinite number of significations, is not unique to language, but is a quality of all human activity. The richness and subtlety of the human world arises from its infinity of significance—as does also its uncertainty, for we can never be sure of the full implications of our actions.

The social world, then, is a world of incipient and actualised meaning; it encompasses the 'tacit cogito', speech and consciousness in all forms, including philosophy. Its institution by and between men is possible because men share an intersubjective basis through their bodily relationship with the natural world. But to say that it is 'possible', because of our intersubjectivity, is not yet fully to account for the creation of the social world. We have yet to examine its genesis. We have not yet answered the question: how does the social world come into existence?

Merleau-Ponty's brief answer to this question is: through the 'work dialectic' (SB 160-84). Perception, our essential way of 'knowing' is, as we have seen, intentional and related to action. It is because we need to use an object, cross a space, climb a hill, that we perceive it as we do. The importance of work is that it creates 'human' objects and a humanised environment for man. It thus inaugurates a new dialectic, between man and a world he *himself* has physically created. By 'work', Merleau-Ponty does not mean simply labour, or economic production. He is using the term, he says, in the Hegelian sense, as '. . . the ensemble of activities by which man transforms physical and living nature' (SB 162). It is his ability to work, his ability to transform nature, that distinguishes man from animals. Animals can adapt their environment, for example when they make nests; some can also use simple tools. For example, a monkey will use a branch as a stick to reach for fruit. But what they cannot do, and what is unique to the work of man, is to 'project' themselves beyond their given environment and create the means to bring their projection into being.

In other words, man alone has a capacity to 'transcend' or surpass the given in creating the social world. This transcendence is two-fold: man transcends nature or the natural world through the 'work dialectic' and he also transcends the social world as it is given at any moment through his capacity to look and act *beyond* the given:

What defines man is not the capacity to create a second nature—economic, social or cultural—beyond biological nature; it is rather the capacity of going beyond created structures in order to create others. And this movement is already visible in each of the particular products of human work (SB 175).

Within this continual creation and recreation of the social world, within the two-fold dialectic of man with nature and man with the social world, consciousness is to be found emerging from the pre-conscious perception of the 'body-subject'. There is no clear boundary between the 'lived knowledge' of the body and the world of ideas. Rather, consciousness is: '. . . a network of significative intentions which are sometimes clear to themselves and sometimes, on the contrary, lived rather than known' (SB 173). Consciousness does not exist just in ideas, but concretely, in the objects men make, in their social and political institutions, in their history.

It is also through the dialectic of work that the essential ambiguity and openness of human existence are revealed. I have already talked about 'transcendence', the process in which men continually go beyond the present they have created. More exactly, transcendence means that endless social change is part of the human condition, that in no area of human life can history come to an end. There is however another pole to the dialectic of human existence: the 'crystallisation' or solidifying of men's projects into concrete traditions and patterns of action which take on their own historical reality and become, in time, an obstacle to that very process of 'transcendence' from which they were born.

Merleau-Ponty often uses the word 'institution' to describe this process (e.g. TL 39–45). 'Institution' is the creation of concretised meanings through a process which is neither conscious 'constitution' nor the working of forces external to man. Instituted meaning arises through the unity of the subjective and the objective, through the unity of man and his world. All human culture and all social institutions arise through this process: political culture and institutions included. But institutions frequently become 'sedimented'. That is, they cease to be appropriate, but from habitual acceptance they gain a place in the pre-conscious intentional structure of society and continue to have a 'weight', a 'privileged position'. In relation to the general social project they become regressive, since they resist change and become obstacles to the 'open' project of human development.

The dialectic of transcendence and sedimentation is an essential element of human existence. Man creates and is then trapped in his own creations. He negates his creations in transcending them—and this process repeats itself endlessly:

> ... the human dialectic is ambiguous: it is first manifested by the social or cultural structures, the appearance of which it brings about and in which it imprisons itself. *But its use-objects and its cultural objects would not be what they are if the activity which brings about their appearance did not also have as its meaning to reject and surpass them* (SB 176).

This is, in a sense, man's burden. But it is also the source of his freedom since it means that the present is not immutable and that man's actions open endlessly on to the future. It is thus to Merleau-Ponty's conception of freedom that we must now turn.

Freedom and History

It could be said that the genesis of human freedom is the central, though implicit, theme of both *The Structure of Behaviour* and the *Phenomenology*. For both works Merleau-Ponty is at pains to reject deterministic explanations of behaviour and to show how it is that man creates his own world. However, the explicit consideration of the nature of freedom does not take place until the final chapter of the *Phenomenology*. It is to that discussion that I now turn.

Merleau-Ponty starts his discussion by considering the traditional debate over free will and determinism, a debate which is central to the split in philosophy between idealism and the kind of philosophy which Merleau-Ponty here calls 'scientism'. The idealists are correct in saying that if man is determined by external factors, in the sense that they 'cause' him inevitably to act in certain ways, then he is a 'thing' and in no sense free. Determinism is unable to account for human behaviour and rests on the myth of the detached observer, the God-like surveying consciousness of the scientist or the philosopher. But if the idealists are correct in rejecting determinism, their assertion—Merleau-Ponty appears to have Sartre particularly in mind here—that man, since he is undetermined, is absoluely free, is also erroneous. Either man is determined, or he is absolutely free; there can be no half-way position, say the idealists (PP 436). Merleau-Ponty, however, regards this as a false choice, forced on us only by the artificial antitheses of idealist and positivist thought. For the 'philosophy of existence', such a choice is not necessary.

The main weakness of the idealist position, that since man is not determined he is absolutely free, is that it empties the notion of freedom of any concrete meaning. By saying that all of each man's actions are free, it makes freedom a 'primordial acquisition', which we all have automatically as part of our essential being: freedom belongs to the slave whether he acquiesces in or revolts against his servitude. In short, the idealist view makes freedom a property of *being*, instead of an attribute of *actions*. It can provide us with no criterion for distinguishing free actions from unfree ones, since it places freedom anterior to action (PP 437). For freedom to have a concrete meaning, it must be an attribute of action and not its non-specific background. Free action must involve choice,[4] but not *any* choice leads to freedom: it must be a choice which leads to 'open' action, action pointing towards the future and transcending the given; action, therefore, which furthers the human dialectic. When a slave chooses to remain a slave, he is making a choice, but it is not one that leads to an open future, to the overthrow of his closed position. It is not a choice that results in freedom.

Since it pertains to actions, freedom has to be considered in its concrete instances. It is, in Merleau-Ponty's word, 'situated' (PP 437, 454). It exists only within a field, a horizon of possible action, within the 'social world' as it exists for particular individuals who already carry within themselves the 'sedimented' weight of their own past, a past which is likely to shape their actions. What distinguishes a free from an unfree action is that it transcends the given, creating an 'open' and not a closed world. But such a transcendence always implies a struggle against the weight of the past and never wholly frees itself from it: 'Our freedom does not destroy our situation, but gears itself to it' (PP 442). The past is lived in our present and generally—though not inevitably—outlines the shape of the future for us. Thus, for example, if I have had an inferiority complex for twenty years, it is 'probable' that I will continue to have it, though never wholly 'impossible' that I should overcome it (PP 442).

What does Merleau-Ponty mean when he talks about freedom creating an 'open' world? We have already seen (p 12) that the concepts of openness and closedness are, in the first instance, related to kinds of perception: hallucinations are proven to be illusions because they are not confirmed in action. 'True' perceptions 'open' on to the world and permit action which confirms them. But openness is a quality, for Merleau-Ponty, not only of perceptions but also of the ensuing actions. Human existence is a dialectic of transscendence, of endless creation and recreation, the continual projection of the present into the future. An 'open' action is one which facilitates the continuation of the dialectic. Based on a 'true' perception, it is capable of widening the field of human action and significance.

Since man is an intersubjective being, an 'open' action

must not only open the horizon for the individual actor, but must *in general* sustain the open dialectic of human existence. As Merleau-Ponty put it in a discussion of the Nazi occupation of France, '. . . one is not free alone' (SNS 142). In a society in which the freedom of some is bought at the expense of the freedom of others, not even those who appear to be free are so. If the human dialectic is based on our shared experience of the natural and social world; if the social world is only possible on an intersubjective basis, we undermine it by denying our intersubjective relations with other groups: there can be no boundaries to intersubjectivity. To make the other—*any* other—an object is to cut oneself off from the world and thus to cut oneself off from the possibility of a concrete freedom in the world. As Hegel showed in his description of the master-slave relationship (the archetype of man's oppression by man) it is the master also who is unfree. The openness of the human dialectic cannot be maintained for some groups through action which oppresses others.

Merleau-Ponty's conception of freedom thus implies necessarily and from the beginning the advocacy of a certain kind of politics which in the late 1940s he frequently called 'humanism' (HT 175–7, 185–7; S 222). This is a kind of politics based on the explicit recognition of our intersubjectivity and interdependence, on 'the recognition of man by man' (HT 186). A politics such as Nazism, which refuses to recognise the humanity of people of a particular race is necessarily non-humanistic and a closure on freedom. Similarly, any politics based on exploitation closes freedom, since it makes an object of the exploited and thus negates intersubjectivity and mutual recognition. Here, I believe, is the link between Merleau-Ponty's 'philosophy of existence' and the political positions—anti-colonialist, anti-capitalist—which he took up as the political editor of *Les Temps Modernes* in the immediate post-war period. Here too is the basis for his adherence to a kind of Marxism in that period, as we shall see.

In a long footnote in the *Phenomenology of Perception*, Merleau-Ponty argues that historical materialism is not to be conceived as an economic reductionism, but as a method for grasping the 'total and concrete existence of society' (172) via the study of the economic. For the economic necessarily includes all other aspects of life, such as the psychological and the cultural, and Marx recognised this fact. Historical materialism is the history of 'social existence'. Merleau-Ponty even goes so far as to suggest that historical materialism can in fact be expressed in 'another language', that of the 'philosophy of existence' (171). For in describing production and productive relations it is in fact describing man's creation of the social world, 'ways of existing and coexisting'.

Already in the *Phenomenology of Perception*, Merleau-Ponty uses this 'existentialised' Marxism in order to exemplify his concept of human freedom. In the same way that the slave can only choose freedom by rejecting slavery, Merleau-Ponty also argues that for the exploited worker freedom can only consist in developing a revolutionary class-consciousness —that is, in recognising the limitations of his life, the 'obstacles' to a free existence that he and others share and then attempting with them to transcend their present situation. The worker's recognition of his class position is not the 'necessary' product of 'objective conditions', as mechanistic Marxism assumes. It is, Merleau-Ponty insists, a 'choice'. But it is not a 'choice' purely at the level of consciousness or reason. Class, says Merleau-Ponty, is neither a pure idea, nor an objective fact, but a mode of existence.

What makes me a proletarian is not the economic system or society considered as systems of impersonal forces, but these institutions as I carry them within me and experience them; nor is it an intellectual operation devoid of motive, but my way of being in the world within this institutional framework (PP 443).

Often class-consciousness, even at the moment of revolution, is more 'lived' than explicitly formulated. A free action is 'open'. It transcends the given, but it can be a leap into the unknown. Thus revolution is more likely to arise from a desire to change a restricting present than from a clearly defined conception of revolution, or of a post-revolutionary society. This does not mean that revolution occurs by hazard; nor does it mean that it is created by the conspiracy of the few. Merleau-Ponty compares the revolutionary movement to the work of an artist. Both are projects in which man asserts his freedom by transcending the present, but without knowing exactly where he is going: 'The revolutionary project, like the work of an artist, is an intention which itself creates its instruments and its means of expression' (PP 445).[5]

In this analogy, as in his discussion so far, Merleau-Ponty would appear to regard individual projects and the projects —or histories—of social groups as essentially the same. But in fact the relationship between individual projects and the social project, or history, is a far more complex dialectic than the analogy would suggest. Every individual has his own history, the temporal development of his existential project. But history in general has its own meaning, its own direction, often differing from individual intentions, so that the outcome of the individual's decisions might not be what he had intended: contingency, uncertainty, are intrinsic to the individual's project. Political action takes place at the meeting points of individual and general history.

Merleau-Ponty insists that history has a direction and a truth. This is possible *because* its prime movers are groups who share a common existential project and act on the basis of their common situation. If history was made by the decisions of individuals not so situated, it would be wholly random and arbitrary. There would be no reason for individuals to remain consistent: the despot might become an anarchist at any moment, if his despotism was purely an intellectual choice and not the expression of his social situation (PP 449). Politics and history must thus be seen as the clash of social forces, not of individual wills; but we must always remember that the social forces come into being only because men, as individuals, share common situations and encounter common obstacles to freedom. Thus the great individual in history is not the one who imposes his will on his times, but the one who takes up what they have to offer. History develops from the initial dialectic between man and the world, in which perception first arises. Like perception, it is rooted in an area of pre-conscious or primordial being, in the mode of the 'One', or 'generalised' existence. But the dialectic of history is two-fold: general history arises from the history of the individual and the history of the individual from general history (PP 450–1).

'The Philosophy of Existence'

History, then, is the field of freedom, in which individual projects attain a general meaning; and in which the individual takes up and transcends the general, his social world. He does this not as an absolute freedom, but from the perspectives provided by his situated existence in the world.

Notes

1 The following comments of Lavelle, written as late as 1939, well illustrate the complacent and introverted nature of the philosophy of this period:

> One cannot doubt that in our country, which is not only that of Descartes but also of the moralists, everyone considers it to be the supreme ideal of existence to acquire the most lucid consciousness of himself and his place in the world, to transform his opinions into clear and distinct ideas, never to agree to anything nor to act except for good reasons, valid for himself and for all, always to seek for the ultimate basis of his knowledge or his action: this is what is correctly called *philosophy* in the noblest and strongest sense we can give the word. (1939, p. v. My translation.)

2 Merleau-Ponty does not use the exact phrase 'body-subject', though he uses similar phrases—e.g. the body as a 'natural subject' (PP 198) and the body as 'the subject of perception' (PP 206).
  The phrase 'body-subject', intended as a summary of Merleau-Ponty's whole conception of the body as the basis of subjectivity and our link with the material world, has been used by Kwant (1963) and by Barral (1965). It is in their sense that I use it here.
3 The Cartesian 'Cogito' is an example of what Merleau-Ponty calls 'a universal constituting consciousness'.
4 'Choice' does not of course have to be a conscious decision; it can also be a pre-conscious willing of the 'body-subject'.
5 Merleau-Ponty's use of the term project here would seem to be slightly different from Sartre's use of the same term. For Sartre, the project is the individual's 'fundamental choice', often made in childhood or youth and then continually reaffirmed in the style of life and action of the individual thereafter. For Merleau-Ponty, although the project involves the choices which ensure the unity or coherence of our actions, it is not based on a single 'fundamental choice' but on the existence of a 'natural self', on which 'my projects as a thinking being are clearly modelled' (PP 440). For Sartre, the project, as a 'fundamental choice', must necessarily be individual, but for Merleau-Ponty, since we are all natural and social beings, the project can also be conceived as a group choice.

2 Merleau-Ponty, Hegel and the Dialectic

As SHOULD already be apparent, the concept of a dialectic is central to Merleau-Ponty's 'philosophy of existence'. It is inherent, for example, in the idea that the 'philosophy of existence' is a synthesis, transcending the alternatives of positivism and idealism. It is also inherent in the explanation of behaviour in the natural world as the outcome of the interaction of organism and environment and in the account of the social world as a process of simultaneous transcendence and sedimentation. Merleau-Ponty rarely talks about his concept of dialectic in his first two books and, moreover, it appears to have somewhat varying meanings. For example, in the interaction of organism and environment, the dialectic is conceived as a 'circular process', a mutually supporting relationship, while in the account of the sedimentation of the social world negation and contradiction are seen as more dominant aspects. But whatever the differing emphases, it is clear that the concept of dialectic is fundamental to Merleau-Ponty's philosophy and that the differences of emphasis do not preclude an essential coherence in the use of the concept.

It appears to have been in the study of Hegel himself that Merleau-Ponty first encountered dialectical thought and it is through the analysis and critique of the Hegelian dialectic that Merleau-Ponty developed his own conception of dialectical existence. In *The Structure of Behaviour* there are already references to the work of Hegel and, in the *Phenomenology of Perception*, critical comments (e.g. pp. 215, 454). In essays written in the late 1940s Merleau-Ponty starts to focus in a more sustained manner on the Hegelian dialectic, arguing in 1946 that: '. . . interpreting Hegel means taking a stand on all the philosophical, political and religious problems of our century' (SNS 63). A distinction has to be made between the way a self-conscious philosopher, such as Merleau-Ponty, explicitly interprets his predecessors, and the way he actually uses them, absorbing their theory, even their style or language into his own work. In this chapter, I want to examine Merleau-Ponty's varying interpretations of Hegel and to try to account for the discrepancies between them. I will also consider Merleau-Ponty's *own* use of dialectical method: what he absorbs and what he rejects from Hegel and what, finally, dialectical method comes to mean in his work.

Merleau-Ponty was not alone in his interest in Hegel, nor in his attempt to synthesise aspects of the Hegelian dialectic with phenomenology and existential philosophy. In France, interest in Hegel was negligible in the first decades of this century. But during the 1930s, as I have already observed, a revival of interest began to take place. Varying and radically new interpretations of Hegel were offered by such writers as Wahl (1929), Koyré (1934), Hyppolite (1935) and Kojève (1962), all of which shared a common interest in linking the Hegelian heritage with the ideas of phenomenology and existentialism, then currently and jointly developing; all of which turned to the study of Hegel's more youthful works as the means of forging this link. It is in the work of Kojève that these conjunctions were most fully developed in the first instance. His series of lectures at the 'Ecole Pratique des Hautes Etudes', between 1933 and 1939, some of which Merleau-Ponty attended (Spiegelberg, 1960, p. 530), appears to have been an initiating event in the development of existential phenomenology in France (Descombes, 1979, Ch. 1).

Merleau-Ponty's Interpretations of Hegel

Kojève focussed in his lectures on Hegel's youthful work, *The Phenomenology of Mind*, and interpreted it as a forerunner of modern phenomenology and existentialism. Hegel, according to Kojève, did not have a dialectical *method*, but simply set out to describe Being, which he found to be dialectical. 'It is only because Being is dialectical that thought—which is Being in the process of self-revelation—is dialectical' (Kojève, 1962, p. 446). Thus, Kojève argues, the Hegelian method is not dialectical but, 'purely contemplative and descriptive, or better, *phenomenological* in Husserl's sense of the term' (p. 447). It is also 'existential' in that it reveals the unfolding of human existence, since this is indissolubly linked to the unfolding of Being.

Merleau-Ponty was clearly influenced by Kojève, but does not fully accept his reading. Kojève makes a phenomenologist out of Hegel by denying that his method is dialectical. By 1945, after his reading of the *Crisis*, Merleau-Ponty, on the contrary, equates Hegel's method with that of Husserl in a directly opposite manner: not by denying the dialectical aspect of Hegel's method, but by claiming that Husserl is *also* a dialectical philosopher. Philosophy (which is to say phenomenology) is not purely contemplative, but also creative. As he wrote in the Introduction to the *Phenomenology of Perception*, 'Philosophy is not the reflection of a pre-existing truth, but, like art, the act of bringing truth into being' (PP xx). Another important divergence between Kojève's interpretation and that of Merleau-Ponty is that the former focusses almost exclusively on the 'phenomenological' Hegel while Merleau-Ponty argued that although the 'young' Hegel can be read as an existential phenomenologist, we need to treat Hegel's life work as a whole and in his later years Hegel became trapped in idealism ending, like Descartes or Kant, by placing the world 'outside' thought, as the object of the philosopher's observation.

Merleau-Ponty's most sustained discussion of the 'young', phenomenological and existential Hegel appears in a critical commentary he wrote on a lecture Jean Hyppolite gave early in 1946 (Hyppolite, 1971, pp. 92–103). Both men in fact focus more on the 'existential' aspects of Hegel's *The Phenomenology of Mind* than on the question of its relation to modern phenomenology. In particular, they argue that the early chapters of the book, describing the development of individual self-consciousness, provide an account of the coming into being of human existence. Hegel might ultimately have been concerned with developing a total philosophical system, but he is equally interested in describing each step in the unfolding of human existence for its own intrinsic significance. As Merleau-Ponty put it, Hegel's *Phenomenology*:

> . . . does not try to fit all history into a framework of pre-established logic but attempts to bring each doctrine and each era back to life and to let itself

be guided by their internal logic with such impartiality that all concern with system seems forgotten (SNS 65).

Merleau-Ponty goes further than Hyppolite in 'existentialising' Hegel by describing the journey to self-consciousness not only in terms of the development of existence, but in the more typically existential terms of 'responsibility' and the 'project': Hegel's thought is existential because it views man as 'a life which is its own responsibility and which tries to understand itself'. The individual 'project' is created in the dialectic between subjective 'self-certainty' and objective truth, as man continually tests his subjective intentions against the world and modifies them. This dialectic must be continuous and unending for man to be man. If ever 'subjective certainty finally equals objective truth' and the 'final stage' of history is attained, 'man, deprived of movement, would be like an animal'. For what distinguishes man is his movement:

... man, as opposed to the pebble which is what it is, is defined as a place of unrest (*Unruhe*), a constant effort to get back to himself and consequently by his refusal to limit himself to one or another of his determinations (SNS 66).

Hyppolite argued in his lecture that in spite of the 'existentialism' of its early chapters, Hegel's *Phenomenology* finally ended up by subordinating individual existence to the Universal, in the form of the march of history towards Absolute Knowledge. But Merleau-Ponty argues that Hegel's idea of Absolute Knowledge should not be conceived as the 'final stage' or 'end' of human development, nor as the closing of the dialectic. It is, rather, a 'way of life', in which consciousness 'at last becomes equal to its spontaneous life and regains its self possession' (SNS 64). Viewed this way, Hegel's notions of History and the Universal can also be regarded as 'existential'. Existentialism is not as individualistic nor as a-historical a philosophy as Hyppolite implies. To move from considering individual self-consciousness to considering a 'universality' based on man's coexistence and the conflict therein, is *not* to cease to be an existentialist. If Hegel's Absolute Knowledge is interpreted as a 'way of life', then the *Phenomenology* in its entirety can be regarded as a work of existential philosophy—although, Merleau-Ponty admits, it is certainly open to other interpretations.

Although the Hegel of the *Phenomenology* can be interpreted as an early philosopher of existence, founder of a man-centred concept of the dialectic, the 'later' Hegel, author of the *Logic* and *The Philosophy of Right*, cannot. This later 'textbook' or 'orthodox' Hegel is an idealist who reduced history to the history of the 'Idea' and who 'found the final synthesis heralded and guaranteed in his own consciousness' (SNS 81). It is in fact to this traditional textbook Hegel, and not to the 'existential' Hegel, that Merleau-Ponty gives most consideration throughout his work. For the traditional Hegel represents the high-point of idealist thought, the unhappy marriage of idealism and the dialectic, from which Merleau-Ponty wishes to rescue the dialectic. Merleau-Ponty therefore repeatedly defines himself against the idealist Hegel, in the process of establishing his own non-idealist position (e.g. PP xix–xx; PP 454–5).

Merleau-Ponty gives us a good general portrait of the idealist Hegel in a lecture written a few years later than his essay on the 'existential' Hegel, his inaugural address at the *Collège de France* (1952). The Hegel in this account fails to realise the limits of philosophy. He does not recognise the fact that philosophy and history are both forms of human practice and that the philosopher is situated *in* history and thus cannot claim to view it objectively. He ends by giving philosophy priority over history—and thus over human existence: '. . . For Hegel philosophy is absolute knowledge, system, totality, the history of which the philosopher speaks is not really history, that is to say, something which one does. It is rather universal history, fully comprehended, finished, dead' (Pr Phil 48).

Hegel sometimes regards the philosopher as the man who simply reads history; at other times he makes the philosopher the subject of history. But either way, 'since history has been staged by him, he finds in it only the sense that he has already placed there' (Pr Phil 49–50). In subordinating history to the Universal, to the 'Idea', Hegel creates a 'dream' of history—and there is no place in that dream for men as individual freedoms, as contingent existences. No longer is Hegel's philosophy the description of human existence. It refuses recognition to existence in the name of its own dream-world intellectual system.

How are we to account for the fact that Merleau-Ponty offers us such divergent interpretations of Hegel? The simplest explanation is, of course, that there really are two Hegels and that Merleau-Ponty is merely being the dispassionate historian in describing both. But on Merleau-Ponty's own admission, it is not possible to be a dispassionate historian of philosophy (Pr Phil 57). Both the idealist Hegel whom the nineteenth century perceived and the existential Hegel the twentieth century perceived are equally real and important to him. To understand this we have to realise that not only is the history of philosophy in the present (as Hegel himself said), but so also is the history of *interpretation* of philosophy: the idealist Hegel whom the nineteenth century saw shares many traits with twentieth-century French idealism. Thus when Merleau-Ponty launches frequent attacks on this Hegel, he is not only attempting to rescue Hegel from himself but he is also participating in a debate with the orthodox French philosophy of his time.

Why, one might ask, is the attack more often levelled through a criticism of Hegel than of Kant, when it was a neo-Kantian orthodoxy which prevailed? Because, I suggest, in Hegel the limits of idealism become most evident: Hegel, unlike Kant, set out to unify theory and practice, reason and non-reason, individual and history. It is just because of these endeavours that Merleau-Ponty regards Hegel as the source of all great modern philosphies:

. . . it was he who started the attempt to explore the irrational and integrate it into an expanded reason which remains the task of our century. He is the inventor of that Reason, broader than the understanding, which can respect the variety and singularity of individual consciousnesses, civilisations, ways of thinking, and historical contingency but which nevertheless does not give up the attempt to master them in order to guide them to their own truth (SNS 63).

But Hegel only starts the attempt; he does not succeed. He *cannot* succeed in integrating theory and practice, individual and history, because he fails to transcend idealism. It is because in the last analysis philosophy constitutes history that Hegel's dialectic remains one of ideas and cannot grasp existence. Modern 'philosophy of existence', having to establish itself against idealism in France, has in Hegel both its main ally and opponent: it is indeed in interpreting Hegel that the 'decisive confrontation' in modern philosophy takes place. Hegel has to be rescued from his own contradictions, through existentialising the dialectic; in the process, idealism can finally be shown to be an inadequate and self-contradictory epistemology, in which the false distinction of subject and object prevents us from grasping the unity of existence.

What then are the grounds on which Merleau-Ponty criticises the Hegelian dialectic? And in what ways does his own use of dialectical method differ from and in what ways does it remain grounded in that of Hegel?

Critique of the Hegelian Dialectic

We have seen that what constitutes human existence and distinguishes man from animal is, in Merleau-Ponty's view, the capacity for transcendence: man continually 'projects' himself into the future and acting in relation to both the natural and the social world, creates meaning only to pass continually beyond it. Flux, creation, the dialectic with the world, are what make man man. This conception of man clearly owes much to Hegel. But Hegel ends by destroying it, subordinating man's existence to the development of the 'Idea'. When the 'Idea' is finally realised, contradiction ceases, history ceases and the dialectic ends in the 'philosopher's dream' of absolute synthesis. The end of the dialectic and the divorce between the philosopher and existence which it implies have various unacceptable consequences, in Merleau-Ponty's view.

1 THE OBJECTIFICATION OF MAN

In subordinating existence to the final synthesis, Hegel finally denies man his negativity and thus his capacity for transcendence. Man ceases to be man, that 'place of unrest', that 'constant effort to get back to himself' (SNS 66). The alternative to man being negativity and transcendence is that man becomes a 'thing', a passive object; and man does indeed become such an object, a victim of the 'cunning of reason', in Hegel's later works. Historical epochs are no longer considered to be intrinsically significant as manifestations of human existence, but are only seen as stages in the development of the 'Idea'; stages in which the men of the time are helpless victims (hence objects) of historical necessity. Thus, for example, in the *History of Philosophy*, Hegel considers Oriental thought only as a moment within the development of the 'Idea'. Since the 'Idea' is said to find its final realisation in Western philosophy, there exists in this work an assertion as to the absolute superiority of Western thought which Merleau-Ponty finds dubious and a failure to consider the intrinsic significance of Oriental thought (S 137).

Hegel's final synthesis not only asserts the superiority of Western philosophy, but also of Western political institutions; for it is in the modern Western state, as described in the *Philosophy of Right*, that Hegel sees the concrete expression of the 'Idea'. Merleau-Ponty does not offer an explicit criticism of the Hegelian notion of the State, but his insistence on an 'open' dialectic in politics must imply a tacit critique. For as the final synthesis, and as a closed static system, the Hegelian State is bound to be repressive; it is bound to reduce men to objects, denying them the further possibility of transcendence.

2 THE DESTRUCTION OF PHILOSOPHY

Hegel's divorce of philosophy from existence does not only have destructive consequences for individual free existence. In asserting the ultimate priority of philosophy, Merleau-Ponty insists that Hegel also ends by destroying the function of philosophy itself. Merleau-Ponty's own attitude to philosophy is not wholly consistent. But what does remain constant in all of his formulations, both those of the 1940s and later ones, is that they see the task of philosophy as clarification. Philosophy *reveals* the meaning of existence; it does not constitute its meaning. This does not mean that it is simply a passive reflection of existence, such as Kojève considered the Hegelian method to be, nor, one might add, that its task is simply to clear up linguistic confusions in our way of talking about the world. Rather, it is a creative activity; it is 'transcendental', since it develops meaning in the course of revealing it. It is 'transcendental' but never autonomous, for it is rooted inescapably and always in our material and social existence. As we have seen, the essence of man, for Merleau-Ponty, is his 'unrest', his continual and contingent movement; philosophy then must reflect and partake of this movement. If it denies it in the name of a rational system, a final synthesis, or some other teleology, it is a denial also of human existence and thus it can no longer perform its task. This is the fate of philosophy in the Hegelian system.

The real philosopher, Merleau-Ponty says, 'does not say that a final transcendence of human contradictions may be possible and that the complete man awaits us in the future' (Pr Phil 43). Such assertions can only be arrived at idealistically, on the basis of a process of logic divorced from existence. The real philosopher stresses the *lack* of necessity in human life: 'He does not place his hope in any destiny, even a favourable one, but in something belonging to us which is not destiny—in the contingency of our history. The denial of this is a fixed (non-philosophical) position' (Pr Phil 44). Thus when Hegel asserts that the development of human history is the unfolding of the 'Idea', he not only subordinates existence to philosophy, but simultaneously cuts philosophy off from its vital roots in existence and destroys its function.

3 SUBJECT-OBJECT DUALISM

Hegel's idealism implies, as we have seen, a subject-object dichotomy. From this stems a further series of inadequacies, in Merleau-Ponty's view. Much of Merleau-Ponty's *Phenomenology of Perception* is taken up with arguing that the split between man as conscious subject—or 'for-itself'—and the world as object—or 'in-itself'—is false, since consciousness is grounded in perception and thus arises from our bodily—i.e. material—existence. Such a subject-object dualism is asserted not only by Hegel, but by all idealists, including those French philosophers in the Cartesian tradition, among whom he numbers Sartre. Hegel in fact attempts to transcend the dichotomy, but fails because of the priority he gives to philosophy (consciousness) over history. It is only when history is completed, when the 'Idea' is realised, that the 'for-itself' takes place for Hegel in the State, but this final unity is achieved only through the denial of our particularity and our finitude; for Merleau-Ponty, on the other hand, the unity of the 'in-itself' and the 'for-itself' is not achieved only with the end of the dialectic, but is a continuous process: 'it is affected at every moment before our eyes in the phenomenon of presence, only to be quickly re-enacted, since it does not conjure away our finitude' (PP 455).

For Hegel, although the 'in-itself' and the 'for-itself' might be unified with the end of history, the existence of the split between them is central to the dialectic until that point: man is pure negativity—the power of consciousness to negate —transforming the world (or being), the object of consciousness. Hegel describes man as 'a hole in being'; but for Merleau-Ponty, man is not pure consciousness, pure negativity: he is material, his 'terrestrial weight', partakes of being; consciousness emerges *from* being and is not in any way opposed to it. Because of its material basis, consciousness can never be complete, but merges with our bodily being. He insists: 'I am not therefore, in Hegel's phrase, 'a hole in being', but a hollow, a fold which has been made and which can be unmade' (PP 215). Consciousness arises within being: their relationship is one of interdependence, not of duality.

Hegel's assertion of the subject-object duality has another consequence. It results in a false description of human relations, since it has to deny the possibility of intersubjectivity. Merleau-Ponty clearly has in mind here the 'master-slave' dialectic, described in the chapter on self-consciousness, in Hegel's *Phenomenology of Mind*: in this account, self-consciousness is said to arise only through the struggle to the death, in which each individual tries to negate the other, to make the other object, in order to affirm himself as subject. Merleau-Ponty argues that the positing of a *cogito*, an individual constituting consciousness, is at the source of this conception of human relations: 'With the *cogito* begins that struggle between consciousnesses, each of which, as Hegel says, seeks the death of the other' (PP 355). For it is only the *cogito* which considers the rest of the world (including other men) as the object of itself. But such a position is, Merleau-Ponty insists, untenable, since to recognise that other men are a threat to me is already to recognise that we share a common ground: 'For the struggle ever to begin, and for each consciousness to be capable of suspecting the alien presences which it negates, all must necessarily have some common ground and be mindful of their peaceful co-existence in the world of childhood'.

The reference here to childhood is highly characteristic of Merleau-Ponty's approach to philosophical issues: individual existence is historical; every man was once a child and the experience that he carries with him through life from this cannot be ignored if we are to understand how he perceives, thinks, relates to others, etc.[1] We can see here the concern with the concrete and with describing totalities which Merleau-Ponty regards as central to the phenomenological method. Hegel and also Sartre—whose account of 'Being-for-Others' in *Being and Nothingness* is closely related to Hegel's account—are guilty of ignoring man's concrete situation and of ignoring his individual historicity in their accounts of the relation of self to other.

The child is clearly neither 'for-itself' nor 'in-itself': he is not a pure 'thing', that is wholly without consciousness, nor yet as self-conscious as is the adult. That we all start life as children, start as such an evident unity of conscious and non-conscious being, is of ontological significance and not a mere fact of biology.

The perception of other people and the intersubjective world are problematical only for adults. The child lives in a world which he unhesitatingly believes accessible to all around him. He has no awareness of himself or of others as private subjectivities (PP 355).

When we reach adulthood, the age of the *cogito*, there is no reason to suppose that we entirely obliterate our childhood thinking: '. . . in reality, it must be the case that . . . the unsophisticated thinking of our earliest years remains as an indispensable acquisition underlying that of maturity, if there is to be for the adult one single intersubjective world'.

Merleau-Ponty's rejection of the subject-object duality as the ontological basis of human relationships has wide political implications. If the necessary relationship between individuals is one of conflict, in which each tries to negate the other, then violence is inherent in the human condition for all times. If this were the case, a politics such as Marxism implies, based on the possibility of co-operation and mutual recognition between men, would be no more than a Utopian dream. It is interesting to note that Sartre had considerable difficulty in trying to reconcile his theory of inter-personal relations with his Marxism. In *Critique of Dialectical Reason*, the schema of self and other from *Being and Nothingness* is to some extent replaced by a concept of intersubjectivity, as a prerequisite to making collective action and communism possible. For Merleau-Ponty the problem does not arise: since human existence *is* intersubjective, since men share a common basis of perception and experience through their bodily insertion in the world, social harmony and community are goals which are in principle attainable. Thus Merleau-Ponty's rejection of the subject-object duality as the basis of human interaction provides the philosophical foundation for his political position.

Merleau-Ponty's Dialectic

If there are no fundamental dualities in being for Merleau-Ponty one must ask how and in what sense the dialectic exists for him. For Hegel, there is a rift between the 'in-itself' and the 'for-itself' which can only be transcended at the end of the process of development of the 'Idea'. But if no such process is necessary, if a Unity exists *prior* to the dialectic, as it does for Merleau-Ponty, then clearly a very different conception of the dialectic is implied.

Briefly, Merleau-Ponty's dialectic differs from Hegel's most fundamentally in the following three ways: (1) It is a dialectic of existence and not as he claims Hegel's is, of ideas only. 'The dialectic', he writes in the *Phenomenology* is 'not a relationship between contradictory and inseparable thoughts; it is the tending of an existence towards another existence which denies it and yet without which it is not sustained'

(PP 167–8). It follows that dialectical thought remains a possibility only as long as it recognises its roots in pre-conscious existence. The notion of 'pure' dialectical thought is self contradictory. (2) It is not a *total* movement; it does not involve the whole of being in one process of development, but concerns tensions, 'contradictions' which are only partial in nature, since they arise within the unity of being. (3) It is a non-teleological dialectic: it moves in no necessary direction, towards no necessary end. It is a tension *intrinsic* to being, as human existence, and would cease if human existence ceased. It is a movement of transcendence in which existence temporalises and creates itself as history but as an infinite and indeterminate history.

The source of the dialectic for Merleau-Ponty is, I have said, being. But being, as conceived in the *Phenomenology of Perception* is a correlate of man and is not prior to him. Being is always being *for* man: and man is conscious being, or existence. Thus man is not, as he is for Hegel or Sartre, the *negation* of being. Furthermore, being is not conceived by Merleau-Ponty as a metaphysical postulate: being is the world. It is the concrete grounding of human life, perception and consciousness. There is a 'primary' or 'primordial' layer of being which is prior to the subject-object duality, since the latter only arises for consciousness, as idea (PP 219).

How then, does a dialectic develop within the unity of being? How do tensions and contradictions arise within it, if it is an essential unity? Obviously there can be no place for a 'first cause' or an 'unmoved mover' to set the dialectic in motion, within Merleau-Ponty's philosophy. There is no motor of rational contradiction, as for Hegel, nor (at this deepest level) of contradiction in the mode of production, as for Marx. Rather, tension is simply inherent in being because it is always being for *man*; man who is finite, but acts and strives to transcend his finitude, in whom freedom and necessity coincide and conflict. It is thus man himself who provides the dynamic of the dialectic; man who brings into being the contradictions of reason and non-reason, truth and error, subject and object, self and other, autonomy and dependence, as he struggles with the world, with the material, spatial and temporal limits which, he discovers, define his finitude. Ambiguity, Merleau-Ponty insists, is 'of the essence of human existence, and everything we live or think has always several meanings' (PP 169).

Human existence, then, is at once constrained and free. This is the paradox at the heart of the dialectic for Merleau-Ponty. Without man there would not be meaning and yet man does not constitute meaning with the freedom of a pure consciousness: he brings forth meaning in a continual process of transcendence, but always bounded by concrete limitations; an endless tension exists between the given and the possible, between as we have seen the 'sedimented' past and the 'open' future.

Merleau-Ponty describes the relations of existence and of transcendence in the following manner in the *Phenomenology of Perception*: 'We shall give the name transcendence to this act in which existence takes up, for its own purposes and transforms a (de facto) situation. Precisely because it is transcendence, existence never utterly outruns anything, for in that case the tension which is essential to it would disappear' (PP 169). An end to the dialectic would thus mean an end to the process of transcendence, and man would become no more than a 'thing', static, passive, a victim of even the most favourable circumstances.

So far, I have been describing Merleau-Ponty's notion of the dialectic in rather general terms; but it is as concrete as it is pervasive for him. It is the source of all culture, all social institutions, all history. It is to be found in areas as diverse as Cézanne's painting (SNS 9–25), our sexual existence (PP 154–73) and the development of communism (SNS 125–36). 'Work', the struggle with and transformation of nature is, as we saw in the last chapter, the originating act of transcendence. But whereas for Hegel 'work' is but a moment in the development of self-consciousness—the means by which the slave achieves self-consciousness (1971, pp. 228–40)—for Merleau-Ponty the work dialectic and man's struggle with nature (which it implies) remain the central dynamic of existence. While in Hegel's dialectic 'work' is only one part of the process of the revelation of the 'Idea', for Merleau-Ponty the dialectic remains *at all times* one of existence, one of men working in and transforming the world.

Given this assertion of the priority of work in creating our world, it is not surprising that Merleau-Ponty ends by identifying his notion of dialectic with that of Marx. Or rather of the 'Young' Marx, who has not yet subordinated dialectical thought to the naive realism of 'scientific socialism', but who deals with the clash of concrete existence in the method of historical materialism and who unifies theory and practice in the notion of 'praxis'. Marxism is not, says Merleau-Ponty, just a materialist transposition of Hegel. Marx does not simply substitute matter for the 'Idea' as the driving force of the dialectic, but places *man* in the centre of the socio-historical process.

'If', Merleau-Ponty asks, in an essay of 1946, 'it is neither a 'social nature' given outside ourselves, nor the 'world Spirit' . . . then what is, for Marx, the vehicle of history and the motivating force of the dialectic?' The answer to this question:

> It is man involved in a certain way of appropriating nature in which the mode of his relationship with others takes shape; it is concrete human intersubjectivity, the successive and simultaneous community of existences in the process of self realisation in a type of ownership which they both submit to and transform, each created by and creating the other (SNS 129).

In this reading then, Marx also takes work—the struggle with nature—to be the source of social life and the dynamic of social change; the Marxian notions of class and class conflict are seen as implicitly existential notions and the class struggle can therefore be described as the dialectical conflict of existences, in which each both sustains and denies the other, and through whose conflict the given situation is transcended.

As I have had to describe Merleau-Ponty's dialectical method rather abstractly in my efforts to reveal it, I will now attempt to concretise it by considering an example of its use—an example which well illustrates the emergence of politics at the meeting point of the individual and the general dialectic. In the immediate post-war period, Merleau-Ponty was much concerned with trying to comprehend what was happening in the Soviet Union and in working out his own position vis-à-vis Soviet communism, the French Communist Party and philosophical Marxism. It is within this context that he wrote the series of essays which first appeared in *Les Temps Modernes* and were then published together, in 1947, under the title *Humanism and Terror*. One of the essays in the series is an essay on the Moscow trials, entitled 'Bukharin and the Ambiguity of History'.

In this essay the problem for Merleau-Ponty is how to make sense of the trial of Bukharin,[2] a trial which appears as a total travesty of justice, within the western 'bourgeois' meaning of the term. For no real evidence is brought to establish that Bukharin *did* plot against the Soviet Union with foreign powers and the charges of Fascist counter-revolutionary activity laid against the old-guard Bolshevik are patently ridiculous, unproven because not proveable. And yet Bukharin himself takes the charges seriously and admits his 'objective' guilt. It is obvious that this superficially farcical trial is the expression of very real conflicts within Soviet society and that Bukharin's position—that his intentions were never counter-revolutionary, but that the effect of his acts was—expresses a real paradox of political action.

It is only within the context of the dialectical relation of the individual to the historical process that we can hope to make sense of the trial. It could not be conducted by the canons of fixed, timeless justice, so revered in the West, because it was concerned with action bearing on the future. It is only from the standpoint of a projected communist society that Bukharin can be judged guilty—and his judges can be no more sure that they are correct in deciding what will assist the birth of this society than is Bukharin. What is taking place at the trial is a struggle between subjective viewpoints, in the face of a given historical situation: 'The Moscow trials only make sense between revolutionaries, that is to say between men who are convinced that they are *making history* and who consequently already see the present as past and see those who hesitate as traitors' (HT 29). In the trial, all the tension and ambiguity of history, of human social existence, are revealed: we see the process of men making history, transcending the present in the name of the future, responsible for their actions and yet never able fully to know the implications of what they do. 'There is', says Merleau-Ponty, 'a sort of maleficence in history: it solicits men, tempts them so that they believe they are moving in its direction, and then suddenly it unmasks and events change and prove that there was another possibility' (HT 40).

Bukharin is the victim of such a 'maleficence'. His acts, caught up by history, transcend his intentions and become counter-revolutionary; and yet they are still his acts, for which he is responsible. In his situation we find epitomised the paradox which I have already said lies at the heart of the dialectic for Merleau-Ponty: man is at once constrained and free. From this it follows that his subjective intentions do not have the objective results that one could expect to follow from them in a world of pure reason. Contingency, ambiguity, the necessary incompleteness of knowledge and reason, all deflect our actions from our initial intentions, while absorbing them within the wider historical dialectic.

Bukharin is a tragic figure in Merleau-Ponty's eyes; a man who carries the paradox of existence within himself and for whom it can only be resolved by death:

> The true nature of the tragedy appears once *the same man* has understood both that he cannot disavow the objective pattern of his actions, that he is what he is for others in the context of history, and yet that the motive of his actions constitutes a man's worth as he himself experiences it (HT 62).

We are not simply dealing here with dualities or alternations of inwardness and externality, subjectivity and objectivity. Rather we are dealing with their synthesis within one person, with 'a dialectical relation, that is to say, a contradiction founded in truth, in which the same man tries to realise himself on two levels'.

Bukharin is not unique. His situation highlights the general contradiction which Merleau-Ponty formulates as follows:

> Man can neither suppress his nature as freedom and judgement—what he calls the course of events is never anything but its course as he sees it—nor question the competence of history's tribunal, since in acting he has engaged others and more and more the fate of humanity' (HT 64).

It would, however, be one-sided to regard this contradiction as tragic only; for its other aspect is that it provides the creative tension intrinsic to human existence. The Russian Revolution has not yet managed to transcend Hegel's 'unhappy consciousness'—man divided within himself—of which Bukharin is a manifestation (HT 67–8). But it contains within it the possibility of an end to class domination and the possibility of a society in which men are in harmony with each other and with themselves.

These are no more than possibilities, in no way guaranteed; if they are to come to fruition it can only be through the continuation of the dialectic of human existence, with all its uncertainties, defeats and bitterness, but also with all its creativity and richness of meaning. Man must always remain that 'place of unrest', which Hegel had described but then denied. If we are to create sense from and for our lives, we must always acknowledge the dialectic of human existence and our own place within it.

Notes

1 Merleau-Ponty develops this line of analysis more fully in the lecture, 'The Child's Relations with Others', published in *The Primacy of Perception*, see especially the section pp. 113–20.
2 Bukharin's trial, in 1938, was part of the series of 'show' trials, starting in 1936, in which were accused (and in most cases condemned and executed) all the members of Lenin's original Politbureau, with the exception of Stalin himself and Trotsky. In all the trials the charges made were extremely vague and general: attempts to assassinate leaders, attempts to restore capitalism, spying for 'enemy' countries. In all the trials the main 'evidence' was the confessions of the accused themselves and the trials were so rapid (for example, Bukharin and twenty others were tried together within the space of eleven days) that there could clearly have been no serious attempt to verify the charges according to normal legal procedure.

PART 2:

TOWARDS MARXISM

3 Marxism and the 'Philosophy of Existence'

MERLEAU-PONTY prefaces one of his essays with the following quotation from Marx: 'To be radical is to seize things by the root. For man, the root is man himself' (SNS 125). The interpretation of Marxism as a humanistic or man-centred doctrine (as opposed to the 'scientific' interpretation of the Second and Third Internationals) has been taking place since the 1920s. It was born in part from an examination of the early writings of Marx, in part as a theoretical basis for a critique of the policies of international communism. In the works of Korsch (1972) and Lukacs (1971) in the early 1920s and of Gramsci (1971) and of the Frankfurt School some years later, Marxism is re-assessed as a philosophic doctrine. It is argued that it is a non-deterministic theory of history, in which the subjective elements of human life, individual and social consciousness in their various manifestations, are seen to interact with the 'objective' elements of social life, the forces and relations of production, in the development of the historical process.

In France some of the early writings of Marx became available with the publication of a translation of them by Molitor in 1927. But the *Economic and Philosophic Manuscripts* were not translated until 1937 and it was not until after World War Two that the philosophical debate about the nature of Marxism, and the challenge to orthodoxy which it implied, began. This debate was not of course due only to the discovery of the 'young' Marx, but also to growing doubts in some sections of the Left about the policies of the Soviet Union and of Marxist orthodoxy, as represented by the Communist Party in France. The debate, not surprisingly, did not begin within the French Communist Party—though it was later to spread there (e.g. Garaudy, 1970). It was initiated by intellectuals sympathetic to Marxism, but outside the Party, one of the principal groups being that of

Merleau-Ponty, Sartre and others connected with *Les Temps Modernes*.

It will already be apparent, at least in part, why in the immediate post-war period Merleau-Ponty considered Marxism to be so important. Marxism provides a humanised and 'secularised' version of the Hegelian dialectic. It too denies the existence of a split between theory and practice, attempts a 'middle way' between idealism and positivist materialism and asserts the inherently social and political nature of human existence. Marxism also thus calls for a positive commitment to political struggle on the part of those philosophers and intellectuals who regard themselves theoretically as defenders of human freedom. As Merleau-Ponty wrote in the first issue of *Les Temps Modernes*, war, the Nazi occupation and the Resistance experience had taught many French intellectuals that they were, inescapably, a part of history (SNS 144–8). Marxism provided a systematic expression of the new experiential truths that Merleau-Ponty and others had discovered during the war years. Many went from the Resistance into the Communist Party.

But for Merleau-Ponty, the Communist Party was not synonymous with Marxism; nor could Marxism be that infallible guide to action and assurance about the future which many in the Communist Party attributed to it. Rather, as Merleau-Ponty described it in the essays mainly written for *Les Temps Modernes* and afterwards published in the two collections, *Humanism and Terror* (1947) and *Sense and Non-Sense* (1948), Marxism was a profound body of philosophical and socio-economic theory, which spoke to the present persuasively, but which was to be assessed on the ground of philosophy as well as action, and from which a politics compatible with the 'philosophy of existence' *might*—but need not necessarily—be developed.

With regard to the politics of the Soviet Union, Merleau-Ponty maintained an attitude of suspended judgement: it might, he argues in *Humanism and Terror*, still contain possibilities for humanistic development; but it might have already destroyed them through repression and dictatorship. It was not yet possible to tell. In the meantime, he says, 'It is impossible to be an anti-Communist and it is not possible to be a Communist' (HT xxi). A cautious 'critical support' was all that could be offered to the Soviet Union and the PCF. It is with an awareness of the 'distanced' nature of Merleau-Ponty's commitment to Marxism that we must approach his attempt to identify it with his own 'philosophy of existence'.

The 'Materialist' Method

One of the main points of departure of Merleau-Ponty's philosophy is the rejection of idealism. For Marx too, idealism was the main philosophical enemy, but in its Hegelian form. In Merleau-Ponty's view, what was important in Marx's relation to Hegel was not the claim to have 'stood the dialectic on its feet', by substituting production for the Idea as the motor of history. Far more important was the assertion of the historicity of all philosophy and the exposure of the main weakness of Hegel: his attempt to make the historical process the object of Mind and to deny his own embeddedness in history (Pr Phil 50).

There is also, in Merleau-Ponty's view, a kind of idealism which pretends that it is not idealism but an objective and scientific method. It remains an idealism, however, because the observer assumes himself to be wholly detached from what he observes and takes up a contemplative stance which implicitly asserts the autonomy of his own consciousness. Such is the materialism of Feuerbach which Marx criticises and such, says Merleau-Ponty, is the so-called materialism of the French Communist Party. He quotes Marx's 'First Thesis on Feuerbach' against the Party. 'The chief defect of all hitherto existing materialism . . . is that the thing, reality, sensuousness, is conceived only in the form of the object or of *contemplation*, but not as human sensuous activity, practice, not subjectively'.

The quotation from the *Theses on Feuerbach* leads us, however, to the question of what Marx's materialism *did* consist in, if it was not the kind of positivistic or 'scientistic' thought that Merleau-Ponty is attacking. Marx never dealt systematically with the concept of materialism. The orthodox view of the doctrine, maintained by the European Communist Parties, has been based mainly on Engels' *Dialectics of Nature* and Lenin's *Materialism and Empirio-Criticism*. This doctrine boils down in the last analysis to an assertion of the primacy of matter over consciousness, of the existence of causal relations in which matter—or the economic base—determines ideological, cultural and other 'superstructural' forms. That Marx criticises such a form of materialism in the *Theses on Feuerbach* is undeniable. A materialism which makes of matter an object of contemplation, detached from and external to man, cannot consistently attempt to make man the agent of historical change. It results, as Marx warns in the third of the 'Theses', in a highly elitist form of idealism:

> The materialist doctrine concerning the changing of circumstances and upbringing forgets that circumstances are changed by men and that it is essential to educate the educator himself. This doctrine must, therefore, divide society into two parts, one of which is superior to society.

While Marx criticises this 'objective' or mechanistic materialism in his early works, it is not certain that he maintained a consistent position throughout his life. In many of his later writings mechanistic overtones are to be found. For example, in the preface to the first German edition of *Capital* (1867), Marx talks of the 'natural laws of capitalist production' and describes them as 'tendencies working with iron necessity towards inevitable results' (1970a, p. 8). Merleau-Ponty was later to argue that Marx's thought contained positivist elements. But in the period with which we are now concerned, until the early 1950s, Merleau-Ponty argues that where Marx talks in such positivist tones it is for polemical reasons only—idealism being his major enemy—and that it should not be taken as a serious shift of position:

> What lends credibility to the legend of a Marxist positivism is that Marx is fighting on two fronts. On the one hand, he is opposed to all forms of mechanistic thought; on the other, he is waging a war with idealism . . . But this struggle against idealism has nothing in common with the positivist objectification of Man (SNS 128).

In Merleau-Ponty's view, Marx's materialism does not consist in any way in an economic reductionism, but in the study of societies or epochs as 'totalities' in which the economic permeates other areas of life but cannot be seen as separate from them or as acting upon them. With historical materialism, he says, economic phenomena provide not a 'cause', but an *'historical anchorage'* for law, culture, etc. (SNS 108). The economic order is the most slow-changing and enduring: 'it is Marxism's way of representing the inertia of human life', it is thus the repository of more general forms of existence, it is where we look to understand the central significance of an epoch: '. . . economic life is . . . the historical carrier of mental structures, just as our body maintains the basic features of our behaviour beneath our varying moods' (SNS 108). What Marx is concerned with then, in Merleau-Ponty's view, is not production *per se*, but production as the manifestation of the varying forms of human existence. Through the analogy with the body Merleau-Ponty also links Marxism with his own concept of the 'body-subject': Marx, like Merleau-Ponty, makes man the *human* subject, rather than the epistemological subject of the historical process (SNS 134).

Insofar as Marx *does* talk about laws of historical development, he is not talking about anything analogous to the laws of the natural world, for the latter are usually a-temporal relations between objects, while social 'laws' are historically situated and mediated by human subjectivity. Thus:

Marx's entire effort in *Das Kapital* is directed precisely to showing that these famous laws, often presented as the permanent features of a 'social nature', are really the attributes (and the mark) of a certain 'social structure', capitalism. . . . A Marxist political economy can speak of laws only within qualitatively distinct structures, which must be described in terms of history (SNS 126).

Thus the materialist method can only be applied *within* historical structures or totalities and it makes no sense to try to analyse matter as prior to or independent of them.

This brings us back to the point Marx had made in the 'First Thesis on Feuerbach', namely that matter cannot be considered independently of or opposed to consciousness, that matter must be 'human matter', matter as recognised and activated by man. Such a materialism, Merleau-Ponty insists, has at its heart conceptions of human freedom and responsibility similar to those of the 'philosophy of existence': it means that in 'praxis', or conscious action, man shapes the material world, that man is the motor of the historical dialectic and that the outcome of history depends on him alone and on no external process. Marxism is thus an 'open' form of materialism, which provides guidelines but no guarantees for the future (SNS 81).

Marx's concept of materialism cannot be considered independently of the theory of *historical* materialism, for as we have seen what is specific to Marx's materialism is its assertion that matter can only be grasped in the historical process, from what Merleau-Ponty would call our 'situation' and that matter is therefore always human matter. Criticising Feuerbach, in *The German Ideology*, Marx writes that 'pure' nature does not exist. Human labour is 'the basis of the whole sensuous world as it exists . . . the nature that preceded human history, is not by any means the nature in which Feuerbach lives' (1965, pp. 58–9).

In its 'positivist' form, historical materialism is the study of the laws of development of social matter, of the process leading to the 'inevitable' collapse of capitalism through its own internal dynamic and the coming of the dictatorship of the proletariat as its necessary sequel. Marx's historical materialism is not of this kind, however, Merleau-Ponty insists: it is a method of studying the historical process in its *totality*, as the development of human existence in all its complexity and variety. It reveals the direction of history not as the unfolding of an 'inevitable' process predicted through the laws of social matter, but as the unfolding of the *inner* logic of history, in which error and contingency always have a part, and in which the outcome of events is never assured. Unlike the Hegelian dialectic, Marx's is an 'open', a manmade dialectic.

As the study of the historical process in its totality, Marxism is in method very close to phenomenology, as Merleau-Ponty conceives it: Marxism too is concerned with the concrete, with particular phenomena, as manifestations of general social existence. It too conceives of history as the dialectical process in which general structures emerge through the interaction of particular interests, institutions and individuals. It too therefore considers all phenomena as having weight and significance within the historical process. Even the crudest 'false consciousness' has to be treated as a manifestation of an aspect of reality. Thus Marxism attempts to penetrate behind 'appearances', and tries to understand them in relation to the total experience of the 'lived world'. As we have seen, Merleau-Ponty even goes so far in the *Phenomenology of Perception* as to suggest that historical materialism could be expressed in the language of the 'philosophy of existence':

> One is tempted to say that it does not base history and ways of thinking on production and ways of working, but more generally on ways of existing and co-existing, on human relationships. It does not bring the history of ideas down to economic history, but replaces these ideas in the one history which they both express, and which is that of social existence (PP 171).

Thus, for example, solipsism cannot be explained as the 'result' of a private property system, but both are aspects of 'the same existential prejudice in favour of isolation and mistrust'. Cultural and economic history are 'two abstract aspects of one unique process' (SNS 107); and that process, which is greater than either, is human existence.

Class analysis, which is of course central to historical materialism, is one of the areas where its 'existential' nature is most apparent, according to Merleau-Ponty. Class is neither an 'objective' reality nor a wholly subjective choice; it is a 'mode of existence'. Class consciousness is not 'caused' (PP 443), nor is it the result of an intellectual choice (PP 447). Rather, class is a mode of being, which can either be experienced 'pre-consciously' or can be consciously articulated. Even in the latter case, for example with the middle-class intellectual who consciously decides to become a revolutionary, it is a question of expressing 'a certain way of being in the natural and social world' (PP 447). Class, then, is a totality, a structure of existence in which all elements of an individual's being, subjective and objective, are found together. Thus the notion of a class that is only 'in-self', (that is, existing 'objectively' but not recognised by its members), must be mistaken within Merleau-Ponty's account. For to assert the existence of such a class is to claim that certain forms exist in history independently of human perception and action. It is to assert that the historical process has its own development, independent of man.

If, as Merleau-Ponty says, Marxism is 'precisely this idea that nothing can be isolated in the total context of history' (SNS 112), it has to admit the weight of ideas in the historical process, even when it thinks them to be mystifications or falsifications. Ideas are never mere epi-phenomena. Marxism cannot—and indeed does not—maintain a distinction between economics as the realm of 'reality' and ideology as the realm of 'appearance': 'The bourgeois ideologies which contaminate all of bourgeois society, including its proletariat, are not *appearances*; they mystify bourgeois society and present themselves to it in the guise of a stable world. They are exactly as 'real' as the structures of capitalist economy, with which they form a single system' (SNS 132).

Philosophy for Marx is also a form of ideology, 'an abstract aspect of total historical life' (SNS 132). Like all such abstractions, since it is part of reality, it contains elements of truth. And according to Merleau-Ponty—and the young Marx—it contains a greater element of truth than other ideologies, since, as self-reflection, it can transcend their mystifications, at least in the realm of thought. But philosophy cannot cease to be an ideology, it cannot cease to be abstract, until it escapes from the world of ideas and becomes *lived*, formulated in action.

'The *cogito*', Merleau-Ponty insists, 'is false only in that it removes itself and shatters our inherence in the world. The only way to do away with it is to fulfil it, that is, to show that it is eminently contained in interpersonal relations' (SNS 133). Hegel's great weakness was to imagine that philosophy could liberate the world. Marx, in his claim that philosophy can only be suppressed through realising it, is asserting the priority of existence over consciousness, while still admitting the centrality of consciousness in the process of human liberation. Philosophy, according to Marx, must be realised as 'praxis', as conscious revolutionary action, or as 'critical thought'. Merleau-Ponty concludes: 'This concrete thinking, which Marx calls 'critique' to distinguish it from speculative philosophy, is what others propound under the name 'existential philosophy'.

Meaning in history

The question of the rationality of history has already been touched upon. The 'positivist' version of historical materialism, paralleling the 'idealist' Hegel, posits laws of necessary historical development, a necessary progression from capitalism to communism, from less to more rational forms of social organisation. In Merleau-Ponty's view, such a conception of history assumes that the historical process is autonomous, a dialectic which is independent of men and which will unfold itself irrespective of what they do. Such a conception is a mystification, for it amounts to a denial of the fact that men make history; it portrays them as the helpless victims of forces external to themselves and returns us in fact to a disguised form of the Hegelian process of the unfolding of Mind.

However, in denying the existence of an inevitable line of historical development, we do not deny *all* sense or shape to history. There *is* meaning in history (Merleau-Ponty uses the word 'sens', which means both meaning and direction); even, we can say, reason (PP 454). But they arise because history is made by men who share a common world, on the basis of that world and not because history corresponds—as Hegel and vulgar Marxists claim—to a pre-determined pattern. There is, says Merleau-Ponty, an *internal* logic to history, as it unfolds event by event. But, 'Every appeal to universal history cuts off the meaning of the specific event, renders effective history insignificant, and is a nihilism in disguise . . . an external history is no longer history' (Pr Phil 52-3).

But how and in what sense does there come to be meaning in history, according to Merleau-Ponty? At the most fundamental level, because as we have seen reason is inherent in the structure of the world as it emerges through our intersubjective perceptions of it. History, as the temporalisation of our world, is thus the repository of meaning: 'Because we are in the world, *we are condemned to meaning*, and we cannot do or say anything without its acquiring a name in history' (PP xix).

Although Marx does not share Merleau-Ponty's concern with the existential or ontological basis of meaning, Merleau-

Ponty argues that Marx's conception of the rationality of history, based on the concept of 'praxis', is not dissimilar to his own. For Marx, he writes, history is:

> the situation in which all meanings are developed, and in particular the conceptual meanings of philosophy, in so far as they are legitimate. What Marx calls *praxis* is the meaning which works itself out spontaneously in the intercrossing of those activities by which man organises his relations with nature and with other men (Pr Phil 50).

Thus reason in history arises through the multiplicity of human action; action which cannot avoid expressing reason since it is human. However, such a reason cannot guarantee definite ends for history. History does not move wholly randomly since it is human, but it moves without necessary ends in sight. Thus error, uncertainty, are an intrinsic part of the historical process. History does not only eliminate the irrational, it also permits the emergence of new forms of it. A wholly rational—and hence static—society is inconceiveable. If the dialectic is to remain a human possibility, it follows that contingency too must always remain: '... the contingency of human events is no longer understood as a defect in the logic of history, but rather as its condition' (Pr Phil 52).

Marx, according to Merleau-Ponty, never insisted that communism was the inevitable end of the historical process, irrespective of what men choose to do. What historical materialism allows us to do is to understand the forces of the present and to project lines of development from our present to the future. But these are lines of 'perspective' or vision, not historical inevitabilities (HT 55); they can form the basis on which we commit ourselves to action, but they do not predict the results of our actions. Thus it is that we have to engage ourselves in the historical process without being sure what the consequences of our acts will become. Thus it is that the Leninist theory of democratic centralism (Lenin being true to Marx in this theory), calls upon the individual to act beyond the bounds of his own certainty, when called on to do so by the Party.

'Praxis'

Following the 'Young Marx', Merleau-Ponty calls the process whereby meaning emerges from history, 'praxis'. 'Praxis' is 'active' reason, as opposed to the contemplative reason of philosophy. For Marx, it is expressed in the revolutionary movement of the proletariat, in which an adequately developed theory (i.e. one which can grasp the reality of the world in a non-mystified form), becomes concretised and further developed in the action of the masses. He wrote in 1844: 'Material force can only be overthrown by material force; but theory itself becomes a material force when it has seized the masses' (1964, p. 52). In 'praxis' the dualities of subjectivity and the 'objective' historical process, of mind and matter, cease to exist, are dialectically transcended. It is easy to see why Merleau-Ponty considers the concept to be of such importance, for it resolves the problems which trouble him as a philosopher of existence; it provides an account of reason in history which is not idealist and it provides a means of admitting the role of subjectivity in history without trapping us in total subjectivism and relativism. In the Marxian concept of 'praxis', man is seen to be the maker of his own world; he is also the source of truth and reason, which emerge only as he makes the world. In short, says Merleau-Ponty, Marxism makes man the 'subject of history' (SNS 80).

It is because it makes man the subject of history that Merleau-Ponty insists that Marxism is, within his sense of the word, a humanism. Marxism implies that history is 'open', made by men, and that its outcome is in their hands (SNS 119). Furthermore, it implies that history can only develop rationally if men are *able* to undertake 'praxis'. 'Praxis', by definition, cannot be blind activity. To engage in 'praxis', meaningfully to engage ourselves in the historical process, we have to ask ourselves what that process is, what forces there are within it, and what our tasks should be. And, says Merleau-Ponty:

> from the minute these questions are raised, one invites the individual to understand and decide; in the last analysis one puts him back in control of his life and agrees that the meaning history will have for him depends on the meaning he sees in it (SNS 79).

Marxists, then, can never consistently attempt to manipulate the masses. The task of revolutionary leaders is to bring the masses to consciousness, to reveal to them their own 'praxis'. In the situation of proletarian dictatorship there have to be leaders to wield effective power against bourgeois elements, but their power must rest on the consent of the proletarian masses, gained through reasoned explanation of their policies (HT 120). It is for this reason that, although Marxism accepts and uses violent means in the class struggle, it alone provides the possible route to a society which will greatly reduce violence in daily life.

Critique of Merleau-Ponty's Marxism

Needless to say, Merleau-Ponty's interpretation of Marxism did not find much favour with the orthodox Marxists of the time. It was vigorously attacked by members of the Communist Party, who regarded 'existentialism' as a philosophy of bourgeois decadence, as 'nihilism', or even as 'Trotskyism' and who did not appreciate non-communists taking it upon themselves to say what Marx had really meant.

While much of the anti-existential literature of the late 1940s simply defamed Merleau-Ponty, Sartre and others and gave no serious attention to their ideas, certain slightly more considered critiques did appear. Of these, perhaps the best of a bad bunch was the book by Lukacs (by then a repentant convert to Stalinism), entitled *Existentialisme ou Marxisme?* (1948), in which he accuses Merleau-Ponty of a devious return to idealism and argues that such concepts as 'being' and 'freedom' are 'supra-temporal' and hence incompatible with Marxism. He also accuses Merleau-Ponty of 'agnosticism' for questioning the existence of a wholly 'objective' direction to history insisting also on the need to examine subjective elements in the historical process. The problem with Lukacs' critique is that it is based on just such a set of crude antitheses—either idealist *or* materialist, either objective *or* subjective—as Merleau-Ponty tries to overcome. Furthermore, it attacks Merleau-Ponty from the standpoint of just such a mechanistic and 'objectivist' materialism as

Merleau-Ponty argues is *not* central to Marxism; a kind of materialism which—ironically—Lukacs had himself criticised so convincingly twenty-five years earlier, in *History and Class Consciousness*.

More justified than Lukacs' so-called philosophical critique is, however, Pierre Hervé's very practical complaint: He reproaches Merleau-Ponty with 'not recognising Marxism at the moment it begins to initiate political action . . . and ceases simply to be a critique' (*Action*, 15 2 46, cited HT 146). For what tend to get lost in Merleau-Ponty's account of Marxism are the centrality of the productive process and the concepts of the class struggle and revolutionary 'praxis'. Although Merleau-Ponty states that 'work' or production is central to human existence and argues that classes are 'modes of existence', he nowhere attempts a phenomenology of either the productive process or class existence. Furthermore, his interpretation of Marx as a 'philosopher of existence' tends to ignore the importance that Marx attached to the analysis of production. It is hard to realise from Merleau-Ponty's account that Marx actually spent most of his creative life working on *Capital*. Merleau-Ponty also tends to forget how important the concept of class struggle was to Marx and that Marx intended his analysis of production to be used as a tool by the proletariat in the conduct of their struggle. Similarly, Merleau-Ponty uses the concept of 'praxis' in a way which empties it of Marx's revolutionary intent. 'Praxis' no longer means, for Merleau-Ponty, the unification of theory and practice in *revolutionary* action, but comes to mean *any* human self-creative activity. Thus language—all language—for example, is seen as a kind of 'praxis' (Pr Phil 54–5), since, like the revolutionary project, it is a process of transcendence, in which meaning always spills beyond its initial boundaries.

Merleau-Ponty is so preoccupied with Marxism as a description of existence—with re-asserting the importance of the concept of totality and showing that there is a full integration of subjective and objective elements in the Marxian view of dialectics—that he forgets that Marx was not developing his theory for its own sake, but as a means towards the overthrow of capitalism. Starting from the standpoint of philosophy, he has a tendency to reduce Marxism to a form of contemplation—in spite of his own assertions that philosophy cannot be divorced from the 'lived world'.

This tendency perhaps becomes comprehensible when we consider more fully the reasons for Merleau-Ponty's interest in Marxism. For although he was also critical of the institutions of liberal capitalism in the immediate post-war period and had been radicalised by the Occupation experience, it would seem to have been primarily as philosophy, and as a possible development of his own philosophy, that Merleau-Ponty approached Marxism. In particular, it seemed to offer him a way of adding a dynamic or historical element to his work. As Sartre summed it up later, through the study of history, which he undertook through the medium of Marxism, Merleau-Ponty moved from a 'static' to a 'dynamic phenomenology' (1965, p. 160).

However, the attempt to merge Marxism with phenomenology cannot, I suggest, be conceived as a matter of simple addition. It must imply a significant modification of both philosophies, if one assumes each to be to any extent a developed and coherent set of ideas. Merleau-Ponty's use of Marxism to enrich phenomenology also implied a modification of Marxism itself—its reinterpretation *as* a form of phenomenological and existential analysis. It is in the process of this reinterpretation that Merleau-Ponty loses the action-oriented thrust of Marxism and, one might say, reduces it to barely more than a dynamic phenomenology. It might well be that we can interpret Marxism as an account of 'ways of existing and coexisting', but it is an interpretation which turns Marxism into a set of *general* statements about human existence *in general*, rather than the prolegomena to revolution which Marx had intended.

Merleau-Ponty's dual attempt—both to 'Marxianise', and thus historicise, phenomenology and to 'existentialise' Marxism—gave rise to serious contradictions in his work. Claude Lefort, one time student and disciple of Merleau-Ponty, points to one of these contradictions when he says that Merleau-Ponty's conception of philosophy was of an endless and multi-faceted process of 'interrogation', while Marxism requires us to choose one particular way of interrogating the world (1963, p. 63). Two different and conflicting conceptions of philosophy are to be found in

Merleau-Ponty's writings of the 1940s. The one, related to his view of Marxism as the completion of phenomenological philosophy, is similar to Marx's own view on the need for a creative destruction of philosophy (1970, p. 136). Thus: '. . . it is true to say that it comes into being by destroying itself as separate philosophy' (PP 456. See also SNS 132–3). The other view, the one to which Lefort refers, sees philosophy as a *continual* process of interrogation, a questioning of existence which can have no end. This philosophy, if it commits itself to any specific action or position destroys itself without fulfilling itself. Thus its relation to action must be one always of scepticism or distance, precluding an adherence to Marxism or any other involved philosophy: 'The fact of the matter is that true scepticism is the movement toward truth' (S 207. Written 1947). Merleau-Ponty's attempts to identify Marxism and phenomenological philosophy uneasily straddle these two differing conceptions of the function of philosophy.

Another, and related, contradiction in Merleau-Ponty's thought concerns his simultaneous assertion that the proletariat are the creators of meaning in history and that *all* men create meaning, whatever they do. For just as it cannot be true both that Marxism destroys and realises philosophy in revolution and that philosophy is an infinite process of 'interrogation', so it cannot be true that *only* the revolutionary class creates historical meaning and that, as Merleau-Ponty argues in the *Phenomenology of Perception*, meaning is inherent in all that we do.[1] Merleau-Ponty oscillates unhappily between a class-based and a universalistic view of existence. Insofar as he manages to reconcile them at all, it is done by emptying Marxism of its class content and turning it into a rather vague and universalistic account of the historical nature of all human existence.

Merleau-Ponty does not appear to have been aware of these difficulties in his thought at the time. He does not seem to have seen that the result of his existential and phenomenological interpretation of Marxism was to undermine its revolutionary intent and to produce major contradictions in his own work. His failure consistently to synthesise Marxism and phenomenology raises for us the question of whether this was his personal failure, or whether the problems inherent in such an endeavour must always result in contradictions or distortions. The issue is still one of debate (see, especially the work of the *Telos* group: e.g. Piccone, 1971; Rovatti, 1970. See also discussions by Mays, 1975 and Smart, 1976) but this is not the place to enter that debate. It is however perhaps worth pointing out that other serious attempts at a synthesis have also ended up either by subsuming phenomenology into Marxism (Tran-Duc-Thao, 1971) or by subsuming Marxism into phenomenology (Paci, 1972). No synthesis has yet been produced which does not subordinate one of the two to the other and which avoids distorting the intentions of both Marxism and phenomenology.

Notes

1 Compare, for example, the following two statements:
   'Marxism is not a philosophy of history; it is *the* philosophy of history and to renounce it is to dig the grave of Reason in history' (HT 153).

   'Because we are in the world, we are *condemned to meaning*, and we cannot do or say anything without its acquiring a name in history' (PP xix).

4 The Critique of Liberalism

SIMONE DE BEAUVOIR tells us in her autobiography that, like herself, Merleau-Ponty had a pious and traditional bourgeois upbringing. Where they differed, however, she says, was in their attitudes to that upbringing: while she always detested it, Merleau-Ponty 'still retained a nostalgia for a lost paradise' (1965, p. 61).

But childhood nostalgia notwithstanding, Merleau-Ponty had, as we have seen, moved towards a Marxist perspective on social and political matters by the end of the war. In so doing, he was obliged to break with many of the values and beliefs with which he had grown up, including those of the liberal political tradition. It was suggested in the last chapter that Merleau-Ponty did not in fact ever *fully* adhere to Marxism and that his relationship to it was somewhat ambiguous. But even so, a considerable rupture occurred with liberalism.

Merleau-Ponty nowhere provides a sustained and systematic critique of liberalism. However, his works contain numerous critical passages from which it is possible to draw together an account of his objections to the liberal orthodoxy which he encountered in French politics. This critique is to be found not only in the essays of the 1940s but also in the writings of the 1950s, such as *Adventures of the Dialectic* (1955), that is writings of the time when Merleau-Ponty was in fact returning towards liberalism but, he believed, to a liberalism significantly different from its predecessors.

Merleau-Ponty's objections to liberalism, from 1945 onwards, go far beyond those of that Marxist rhetoric which simply dismisses liberalism as a ruling-class ideology and a sham: unlike the Communist Party Marxists of his time, Merleau-Ponty clearly believes that liberalism, even if it is inadequate, is worthy of serious discussion. As a phenomenologist, Merleau-Ponty insists that *no* phenomena can be *a priori* excluded from examination as being unnecessary for our understanding of the world. Thus he believes that if we are to understand our present society, an examination of liberalism is necessary *because* it is the dominant ideology, and not in spite of that fact; for an ideology has a real weight in history. Ideologies are not disembodied systems of ideas; nor are they mechanical reflections of economic realities; rather, they are ways of existing and acting. To be a liberal is not just to hold certain beliefs; it is a way of perceiving and a way of being in the world.

But it is a way of being which, Merleau-Ponty believes, fails to apprehend reality sufficiently fully to be a basis for effective political action. For it refuses to recognise the complexity and ambiguity of human existence, the context within which all political actions must make sense. In particular, it insists on seeing politics in simplistic terms in which contingency has no place and in which reason, order and harmony are believed naturally to predominate. For the liberal, it appears there are no problems about politics: politics should be conducted according to the principles of justice, and the individual's conscience is clear, whatever the consequences of his acts, so long as he has proceeded by such principles. For that great liberal, Alain, Merleau-Ponty says, the main precept was 'do each day what is just, and do not worry about the consequences' (AD 25). But politics is not as simple as Alain's maxim implies: we have to distinguish decisions from events; the outcome of just decisions need not be just events, given the complexity, contingency and incipient violence of politics.

At the risk of being a little over-schematic, I will divide Merleau-Ponty's criticisms of liberalism into two groups: those which deal with it primarily as a system of ideas, as a philosophy, and those which deal with it on a more ideological level, as it is used, and has been used, to justify actions. However, it must be pointed out that even the 'philosophical' criticisms, which I will consider first, are not made at the level of pure theory. For philosophy, Merleau-Ponty insists, is not an activity centred in itself, but one which questions the world around the philosopher: it is, in short, a phenomenological activity. It is not just permissible but is *necessary* that the philosopher should start from his own experience of the world and not from abstract problems. It is thus from his own personal experience of its limitations that Merleau-Ponty begins his critique of liberalism. It was, he says, the experience of the German occupation of France which first taught him, and many of his generation, how limited was the set of beliefs with which they had been raised. After the war, it was the role that he saw liberalism playing in the defence of colonialism and the Cold War which led him further to develop his critique of it.

Liberal Philosophy

In 'The War has Taken Place', Merleau-Ponty discusses the failure of liberalism to provide guidelines for French intellectuals, such as himself, in the face of the Nazi occupation. In his view, liberalism is more than a set of values or beliefs about politics. It contains, implicitly or explicitly, a whole conception of human relationships and of man's relation to the world, a certain set of epistemological and ontological presuppositions, a general perspective on human existence, on which its analysis of politics and history is based. Merleau-Ponty describes this perspective as the 'Cartesian' conception of politics (SNS 146). It sees the world as the sum of individual consciousnesses; freedom as consisting in individual acts of judgement and will. Politics is thus an area of individual moral decisions, essentially rational and to be comprehended in terms of the ideals that men pursue. For such a conception of politics, Nazism and all other apparently irrational forms of politics are hard to explain. They can only be explained as 'accidents', as unfortunate and abnormal intrusions into a world that is normally rational.

But, Merleau-Ponty insists, the violent and the irrational are not exceptions in politics. They are a large portion of the stuff of which it is made, not just because of the existence of class conflict, which he believed Marx had amply demonstrated, but also because politics takes place in the flux of history, where the outcome of events can never be predetermined and human will is continually deflected. Alain's 'do each day what is just' is a maxim which ignores the temporal—and hence contingent—dimension of politics and the fact, recognised by Machiavelli, that 'in historical action, goodness is sometimes catastrophic and cruelty less cruel than the easy going mood' (S 216). An account of politics which ignores such factors cannot provide an adequate explanation of the normal course of political events, let alone of the excessive irrationality and violence of the Nazi regime. The Cartesian liberal could label Nazism as evil or call it enigmatic or abnormal, but he could not *explain* it.

Nor was liberalism any more satisfactory as prescription. It was unable to provide the ethical guidelines the intelligentsia needed, since it failed to acknowledge their problems: what relevance could precepts such as Alain's have in a situation where, simply by continuing to live, one was forced constantly to cooperate with and, in practice, to sustain the Nazis? No one could keep their hands clean—the political and the personal were, as they had always in fact been, too intertwined—and a political position based on the assumption that one could do so was evidently naive or dishonest. Liberalism was no more adequate on a prescriptive than on an explanatory level.

Its inadequacy is closely connected, according to Merleau-Ponty, with its idealism, with its attempt to understand the world in terms of ideas and values alone. Politics is not about values alone; it is a realm of the factual, of events and configurations which are not purely the products of consciousness. Our values are formed in the continuous dialectic of consciousness and the factual world. But they do not produce that world any more than it produces them; both sustain and interpenetrate each other. In its attempt always to confront situations with values alone, in its pursuit of the 'politics of understanding', liberalism denies the dialectic in which both values and the 'factual situation' are born (AD 5).

Another way of expressing this criticism is to say that liberalism is a-historical: it does not question the source of its own values, nor consider their changing significance in history. Instead, it assumes its principles to be universal, applicable to all times and places, because they are 'true'. It was this illusion which the German occupation shattered. Freedom, which had seemed to be an attribute of individual consciousness, was shown to be dependent on social conditions. Even those intellectuals who withdrew into their own private world of writing or painting and were not directly molested by the Germans, knew they were not free; they learnt that they were circumscribed by the limitations placed on others; they learnt that: 'their former freedom had been sustained by the freedom of others and that one is not free alone' (SNS 142).

The belief in individual autonomy, which the Occupation destroyed, was a belief that had always been, to some extent, illusory. Merleau-Ponty does not say that the liberal values are wholly empty, but they have often been so formal, abstract and so divorced from social reality as to have been irrelevant to most people, either as a description of how politics is conducted or as a set of criteria for their own actions. 'We were not wrong, in 1939, to want liberty, truth, happiness, and transparent relations among men', he says, but what the war and the occupation taught was that 'values remain nominal and indeed have no value without an economic and political infrastructure to make them participate in existence'. He concludes: 'It is not a question of giving up our values of 1939 but of realising them' (SNS 152). They must become *lived* values, embodied in the structures of daily life and cease to be intellectual abstractions.

The a-historical nature of liberalism is also apparent, Merleau-Ponty thinks, in the kind of attacks being levelled at the Soviet Union in the post-war period. It is undoubtedly true that Soviet politics do not conform to the values of Western liberalism, that Russia is not democratic in the Western parliamentary sense, that certain individual freedoms, valued in the West, are not protected there. Merleau-Ponty does not condone these omissions. But neither—unlike the liberals of the time—does he argue that because of them the Soviet Union must be a wholly coercive, unfree society: it *could be* that it is so; but the question has to be answered through a careful study of the society, through a study of 'human relations' in the Soviet Union, and not through the application of external and abstract criteria. To condemn Russia out of hand for a failure to live up to Western liberal principles is to refuse to make any effort to understand her, to assume that liberal values are universally valid and that freedom can be attained through them alone.

The problems which liberalism runs into, insofar as they are methodological, stem from the epistemological errors of idealism. I have so far described two kinds of error. Firstly, the perception of politics as primarily a realm of values, with its consequent assertion that political actions have always to be judged by moral criteria. Secondly, the a-historical nature of liberalism, evidenced in its belief that its principles have a universal validity. Both these errors are, for Merleau-Ponty, aspects of a more general kind of error: that of being 'abstract' or undialectical. To understand this criticism fully, one has to go back and examine Merleau-Ponty's conception of phenomenology as a way of knowing which embraces 'totalities' and comprehends them dialectically.

In its return to the 'things themselves' phenomenology is a method which refuses to impose external categories on experience—'The real has to be described, not constructed or formed' (PP x). Thus, when we study any phenomenon, be it a sea-shell (Bachelard, 1949, Ch. 5) or politics, we cannot in advance determine what the edges or boundaries of the phenomenon will be. They must be free to emerge as part of the total configuration which is the phenomenon for us, in the dialectic between us and the world in which our perceptions and conceptions are born. From this approach it follows that we cannot clearly delimit politics (or free or democratic politics); that it might spill over into economics, family life, religion, myth etc. and that the core of the phenomenon which is politics will vary from society to society. (For example, the Church was a major 'political' institution in medieval society, but has ceased to be so in industrial society). Thus it becomes impossible to identify politics exclusively with the institutions of and activity surrounding the Western liberal-democratic state.

Furthermore, it becomes evident that values and moral precepts and their relations to politics can be in no way fixed or universal. A phenomenology of politics must seek to describe the emergence of values and their interplay with politics within the historical process. Values are seen to emerge and change within history and we have no reason for assuming that the values of our own time and place are in any way superior to, nor our conceptions of society any more true, than those of other peoples. This is not to say that Merleau-Ponty advocates a position of total relativism: the essence of man is his 'openness', his capacity for transcendence, for continually going beyond his given 'situation';

since man is a free 'project', those societies are preferable which least trammel the creative dialectic of existence. Such societies cannot, however, be identified *a priori* with any set of intellectually articulated values. If we are to know them, it can only be done experientially, through a process in which we 'bracket' or suspend our own intellectual preconceptions.

For Merleau-Ponty, as for many Marxists, values and ideas are seen emerging and developing in action, and as expressions of our material existence. But for Merleau-Ponty, unlike most Marxists, it is not just the experience of the material world of labour and production, but equally our bodily perception of the world, the pre-conscious 'knowing' of the 'tacit cogito', which provides the ground from which we create our values. Liberalism refuses to recognise the pre-conscious, the obscure, the half-submerged aspects of life. It insists on the autonomy of consciousness and denies its bodily roots. It perceives the world from the standpoint of logic and attempts to impose on the world principles which do not derive from the world as it is, but from a rationalistic idealisation of it. As such, liberalism is doomed to remain abstract and undialectical and, as a conception of the world, incompatible with the phenomenological philosophy which Merleau-Ponty defends throughout his work.

It might well be objected that Merleau-Ponty paints a very over-simplified picture of liberalism and that few, if any, liberals fit his description. It is an inconsistency in Merleau-Ponty's method that he does not discuss the work of individual thinkers: to describe an 'ideal type' liberal philosopher, without describing the ideas of particular thinkers is not to engage in the detailed study of concrete phenomena which he advocates elsewhere as the essence of correct phenomenological method. The only thinker Merleau-Ponty does briefly mention by name is Alain, and a possible explanation for his lack of detailed discussion of other writers is the fact that Alain dominated liberal thinking in France in the inter-war years. Through his daily 'Propos', appearing year after year in the press, Alain (1868–1951), moulded the opinion of the 'middle' classes in France—the small businessmen, the clerks and minor bureaucrats, the teachers, the more prosperous sections of the peasantry—for several decades. The Radical Party, whose acknowledged theorist he was, was almost continually in office for the first forty years of this century. For Merleau-Ponty's generation, liberalism *was* Alain. It is perhaps for this reason that it seemed to him unnecessary to differentiate more finely between different liberal thinkers or schools of liberalism.

If this is the case, we must then ask how well Merleau-Ponty's description of liberalism fits Alain's doctrines. It is in some ways an oversimplification. For Alain does not deny the importance of bodily, or what he calls 'animal', needs. Nor does he assume that politics is a realm of order and principle. On the contrary, politics is the struggle to impose the 'spiritual' on the 'animal' in man. But Merleau-Ponty is correct to point to a profound mind-matter dualism as the basis of Alain's philosophy and is correct to criticise him for idealism since he asserts the ultimate autonomy and superiority of the 'spiritual' (see, for example, 1956, Vol. 1, pp. 981–3). The basis of his liberalism is the call for a minimum role for the state as a prerequisite for individual moral development: moral development consists in *self*-discipline, *self*-regulation of the 'animal' in us. Hence all state intervention is an evil, even though it is sometimes necessary, and all power is corrupting.

Alain maintained a dogged insistence on this position even at the time of acute economic depression in the early 1930s — at a time when in Britain mainstream liberalism was already on the way to accepting Keynsian economics and welfarism. Small wonder then that, for Merleau-Ponty, liberalism, as epitomised by Alain, seemed to consist in the subordination of the very real needs of millions of people to a set of abstract principles. In practice, the subordination of the 'animal' to the 'spiritual' meant the acceptance of widespread unemployment and misery.

Liberal Ideology

If liberalism was simply an over-abstract way of conceiving politics, one more example of the inability of non-dialectical thought to grasp the full complexity of the world, then the matter could be shrugged off as being of interest to no one but philosophers. But as the example of Alain itself suggests, this is not the case: liberalism has been the dominant political ideology of the West since the end of the eighteenth century. In its name wars and revolutions have been made and violence justified. In its name, in the late 1940s and the 1950s, the Cold War was being defended and the attempt to suppress colonial liberation struggles in Indo-China and North Africa was being excused. The inability of liberalism, as philosophy, to grasp political reality, renders it dishonest and, Merleau-Ponty suggests, liable, as a political doctrine, to be used to disguise or exonerate the aggressive interests of Western capitalism.

The dishonesty of liberalism stems primarily from its refusal to admit the fact that politics is, at least in part, a realm of incoherence, of contingency, of struggle—hence of violence—and that it is not a realm of principles alone: 'History', says Merleau-Ponty, 'is a struggle and politics a relationship to men rather than principles' (S 219). To talk of principles alone is to condone violence without admitting to the fact. To defend formal liberty is often, in practice, to defend oppression, since formal rights and formally democratic institutions can have little meaning to the physically oppressed. Since man is not a pure consciousness, but a *bodily* existence, freedoms that operate at the intellectual level only can be of only secondary importance as long as the well-being of the body is neglected. This is not to say that such liberal freedoms as freedom of speech are a 'sham', but they are somewhat empty and irrelevant freedoms to those, like the unemployed of 1930s' France, who lack their basic material requirements. Furthermore, it has been in the name of liberty that wars which have impeded liberty have been fought. For example, it was in the name of justice and freedom that the soldiers of Revolutionary France went to put down the slave rebellion in San Domingo, led by Toussaint Louverture (S 220); while at the time Merleau-Ponty was writing, the interests of imperialism were being militarily defended in Indo-China and elsewhere in the name of freedom, the defence of the 'free world' (HT xiii–xiv).

Liberalism, then, threatens to become more than just a tacit acceptance of violence. It can become what Merleau-Ponty describes as 'an ideology of war' (HT xxiv). It is such a liberalism which becomes an apologist for Western capitalism and refuses to understand or to enter into dialogue with the Soviet Union. It condemns the Soviet Union from the ground of abstract freedom and gives rise to the possibility — a possibility much discussed and feared in France in the late 1940s — of a third World War which, unlike the fight against Nazism, could be in no way progressive (HT 181–2). If we are to understand the Soviet Union and avoid war, it is necessary to expose the hypocrisy and abstractness of liberalism and to develop alternative criteria to liberal principles by which to assess the Soviet and other political systems.

It is as a preliminary to this undertaking that Merleau-Ponty develops, in the Preface to *Humanism and Terror*, a distinction between two kinds of liberty, between the abstract or formal liberty so dear to the liberals and a form of liberty more deeply rooted in our existence. The latter, which he describes as 'concrete liberty' (HT xxv) or as 'practical freedom' (HT xxiv), can only be understood phenomenologically, that is, as it is experienced. We have to distinguish between liberty as a concept and liberty as it is lived. The error of the liberal is that he ignores this distinction by naively assuming that where liberal ideas are expressed or institutionalised, freedom automatically exists. In the process he often destroys lived freedom because in his dedication to the principles he is prepared to trample on individuals. Liberty becomes 'a false ensign . . . as soon as it becomes only an idea and we begin to defend liberty instead of free men' (HT xxiv).

But what then is the alternative to this abstract and dangerous conception of liberty? Unfortunately Merleau-Ponty gives us only a rather schematic idea. The alternative is, he suggests, a liberty which acknowledges its roots in our pre-conscious existence and which develops within the internal dynamic of existence, accepting its given reality, instead of forcing it to conform to idealisations. Freedom, if it is to exist, must not ignore the non-rational, the contingent, the violent. It has instead to absorb them somehow into its own self-development.

What, however, is not immediately apparent in Merleau-Ponty's account is *how* freedom is to absorb these aspects of life, what concrete liberty is *like*, or how we can recognise it. When Merleau-Ponty discusses the liberal dismissal of the Soviet Union, he is surely correct to point out that one cannot *a priori* dismiss the possibility that freedom exists there, simply because the liberal canons of freedom are not followed. But what is less evident is how, in fact, one could discover whether or not it exists where Merleau-Ponty insists that it should—in human relations.

Clearly one cannot answer this question simply on the basis of subjective opinion or feeling. As we have seen, the slave who 'chooses' to remain a slave is not engaging in a free action. A free action provides 'open' possibilities for the future, allows the continuation of the dialectic of human creativity and thus has a 'weight', or significance, in history. Concrete freedom cannot, then, be recognised on a wholly subjective basis, any more than it can be recognised by applying 'objective' liberal principles. Instead, it has to be sought for in the *total* structure of society, the unity of subjective and objective elements.

By 'human relations', Merleau-Ponty means considerably more than individual interpersonal relationships: 'human relations' are not just those ways in which people interact directly with each other, but also the ways in which they create the human world and relate to each other through its mediation. Thus, language and the organisation of production are both kinds of 'human relations', as are political and legal systems. In such 'human relations' subjective and objective, the immediate and the historical, meet. It is thus to all the 'institutions' of a society, considered as historical structures and as mediations of human existence, and as either furthering the dialectic of existence or closing it, that we must turn, to discover concrete freedom, or its absence.

To discover whether or not concrete freedom exists in a society, we must consider it as a totality of interrelated structures or institutions; we must ask whether these institutions provide the possibility of the furtherance of the human dialectic, or whether they limit the general human dialectic. It is on the basis of such questioning that Merleau-Ponty concluded in 1947 that the Soviet Union might be more free than the Western liberal regimes, in spite of its lack of certain kinds of political freedom. The main reason for optimism was the alteration that had taken place in the organisation of production in the Soviet Union: relations between men concerned with their fundamental life activity, 'work', were no longer based on exploitation and unequal ownership. This, Merleau-Ponty believed, must mean that the potential for individual and social creativity, i.e. freedom, was considerable.

When, by 1950, with evidence of the Soviet Labour camps, Merleau-Ponty began to change his opinion on the Soviet Union, it was for related reasons—not because of the lack of liberal or constitutional freedom, but because collective production was now evidently not a means to 'open' human relations: it had become an excuse for oppression and the justification of a 'cruelly hierarchical society' (S 265), even of slavery. The future was no longer open; 'human relations' were now subordinated to production; the subjective was being sacrificed to so-called 'objective' economic development; the dialectic of subjective and objective, in which concrete freedom is to be found, had been ruptured.

This later critical attitude to the Soviet Union did not lead Merleau-Ponty to retract his critique of liberalism. He comments: 'The decadence of Russian Communism does not make the class struggle a myth, "free enterprise" possible or desirable, or the Marxist criticism in general null and void' (S 269). A littler further on he adds:

A society is responsible for everything it produces, and Marx was right to reproach liberal thought, as for an accountable fraud, for the artifices by which it puts unemployment, colonial labour and racial inequality beyond accountability by imputing them to nature or to chance (S 270).

Some Comments on Merleau-Ponty's Critique

I have already suggested some of the weaknesses of Merleau-Ponty's critique of liberalism in my account of it. Since I have only drawn together arguments from different places in his writings and Merleau-Ponty did not attempt a rigorous critique of liberalism in any one work, one cannot protest at the lack of rigour in the account I have presented. Even so, there are certain criticisms to be made. These concern the narrowness and simplicity of the concept of liberalism which Merleau-Ponty uses and his apparent indifference to its historical dimensions.

Merleau-Ponty discusses and criticises idealism, which he

regards as the philosophical basis of liberalism, at length in several of his works. It is frequently in opposition to idealism that he defines and defends phenomenological method, arguing that it alone can resolve the problems of idealist philosophy. Thus when he criticises liberalism by saying that it is a form of idealism, there is a fully developed critique behind that assertion. If liberalism is a form of idealism, he has already shown elsewhere the philosophical difficulties that it must encounter.

While Merleau-Ponty's critique of idealism would appear to be in large part valid, it is perhaps necessary to ask here just how far the term is appropriate to liberal philosophy in France. Clearly the term can be applied to the kind of liberalism which Merleau-Ponty describes as 'Cartesian' politics, that liberalism which sees politics only in terms of individual moral decisions. But it is not an adequate description of other major strands of French liberal thought, from the eighteenth century onwards, which have been empiricist and utilitarian in character (see, for example the works of Helvétius, Montesquieu and de Toqueville, to name but a few). It would appear to have been only from the beginning of this century, when a movement of reaction against positivism generally revived idealist philosophy in France, that liberalism began to conform more fully to Merleau-Ponty's description of it (see, for example, as well as the works of Alain, Brunschivg, 1931, Ch. VI).

Repeatedly throughout Merleau-Ponty's work, one finds an insistence on the historicity of human existence and on the situational nature of knowledge. Yet, when he comes to describe liberalism, he shows no awareness of its genesis or of its historical development. It appears, in his accounts, to have emerged fully-fledged in its French twentieth-century form, out of the void. Not even its relationship to the Cartesian philosophy on which it is said to be based, is ever demonstrated. Nor are the changing economic and social conditions with which its development was connected ever discussed. A consequence of this a-historical approach is that Merleau-Ponty condemns liberalism as if it had always played the role it was performing when he was writing—the role of a hypocritical defender of ruling-class interests. But this has not always been the role of liberalism. There have been periods when it has been a force for what Merleau-Ponty would consider progress, when its demands for such freedoms as religious toleration or for due process of law have been demands truly to enlarge the scope of human actions, to extend the horizon of possibilities of the individual project. Indeed, Marx, whose analyses form part of the basis of Merleau-Ponty's critique, was always ready to admit that capitalism had been, in its time, a force for human liberation (e.g. 1971, p. 111) and that its liberal political forms could provide a possibility of real advances for the proletariat (e.g. 1973, p. 109). It is ironic that Merleau-Ponty, who criticised the Marxists of his time for their gross oversimplifications should neglect such positive aspects of the history of liberalism, ironic that he should see it only through the eyes of his present and as if eternal, when what is in general central to his philosophical method is the stress on the fluidity and historicity of human existence.

Another serious flaw in Merleau-Ponty's treatment of liberalism is his insistence that it denies the existence of the violent or the irrational in politics. This is simply not the case. Alain's views are surely typical of those of most liberals, from John Locke onwards: there is a battle between the forces of animality, which are irrational and violent, and those of consciousness, which endeavour freedom and harmony. It is only because there are these two conflicting forces in human life that the state, as an organ of control, is necessary. The problem for all liberals is, having admitted the need for the state as a coercive force, how to control it. The only people who in fact hold the view which Merleau-Ponty attributes to liberals are anarchists who—quite consistently—assert both that there is no *necessary* realm of violence and irrationality and that the state is unnecessary. But clearly liberalism is not anarchism and its recognition of the need for the state is evidence of its recognition of the existence of violence and irrationality and of the need to use organised force to contain them.

Had Merleau-Ponty restricted his criticisms to the liberal's refusal to see economic exploitation as violence, or to commenting on the rigidity of the distinction which liberals so often make between the realms of reason and unreason, realms which in both individual behaviour (SB Ch. 3) and in history (SNS 3–5) are not always clearly distinguishable, his case would surely have been much stronger. But as it is, Merleau-Ponty erects much of his critique on claims which any close study of liberal theory will show to be indefensible and, more importantly, presents such a schematic and a-historical account of liberalism as to constitute an abandonment of his avowed interest in revealing the lived world, in describing existence in its concrete forms.

5 Truth, Morality and Violence in Politics

The Possibility of Moral Action

THE order of truth and the order of violence are discrete and yet imply each other. As we saw in the last chapter, the core of the problem of the possibility of morality in politics is, according to Merleau-Ponty, to be found in this disjunction. In its naive forms, such as Alain's, morality is the attempt to apply the order of truth to the order of violence. Any attempt which goes beyond such naivety must grapple with the disjunction, as both Marxism and existential philosophy have discovered.

Before examining Merleau-Ponty's considerations of these intertwined issues of truth, morality and violence, a preliminary question needs to be asked: how important is the issue of political morality for Merleau-Ponty? Sartre, it appears, abandoned his plans for an ethics as a sequel to *Being and Nothingness*, asserting that '. . . Ethics is a collection of idealist tricks intended to enable us to live the life imposed on us by the poverty of our resources and the insufficiency of our techniques' (cited in de Beauvoir, 1965, p. 218). Since Merleau-Ponty never wrote a systematic work on ethics *per se*, one is justified in asking whether he too thought ethical questions to be irrelevant.

Certain passages in his work certainly appear dismissive of the question of morality, especially in relation to politics (see, for example, SNS 103 and SNS 153). However, a careful reading of such passages suggests that this is not the case: what Merleau-Ponty is criticising is a particular *kind* of morality which, because it is too abstract and simplistic, fails ultimately to achieve what it attempts, the treatment of men as ends. It is the kind of morality which goes hand in hand with liberalism and which cannot effectively bear on politics because it proceeds from a faith in the universal possibility of justice, and not from an examination of the real world.

The rejection of such abstract morality is not however the rejection of all morality. The possibility of moral action is not assured, in Merleau-Ponty's view, but that is not to say either that morality is impossible or unimportant—far from it. The problem of moral action is not one for politics only, but is rooted in the fundamental ambiguity of human existence, in the fact that we are simultaneously unique individuals and part of a wider social generality. Merleau-Ponty's treatment of the problem arises directly from his account of existence in the *Phenomenology of Perception*: since we each perceive from our own individual situation and since the overlap of perceptions must be the basis of all forms of intersubjectivity, the question of morality is also inseparable from the question of perception.

In a lecture of 1946, 'The Primary of Perception and its Philosophical Consequences', Merleau-Ponty makes this connection very clear. After rejecting the ethics of abstract principles and arguing that we must also be concerned with the consequences of our acts for others, Merleau-Ponty locates morality in the matrix of our perception of others and the possibility of agreed perceptions. However, on this basis, we cannot be assured that morality is possible. Rather, '. . . it appears possible that our relations with others are involved in immorality, if perchance our perspectives are irreconcilable' (Pri Per 26). This does not however entitle us to become cynics or sceptics and wholly to reject the possibility of morality. For while providing no absolute guarantees or certainties, perception does *in general* provide the basis for intersubjectivity: (see PP 351–2 and 448) and thus the possibility of agreed values and truths. Morality then is possible on the basis of our perception of the other and our common situation, but it is not assured and it ceases to exist on those occasions (for example in war, Pri Per 35) when we refuse to recognise that others are in a common situation with us.

Merleau-Ponty's remarks in this lecture are not related specifically to politics, but they obviously apply to politics as a particular area of activity within the general human world he is describing and, moreover, an area which has the distinctive feature of involving the use of violence. Even a moral politics must, paradoxically, do violence. We need to explore this paradox, but before doing so it is necessary to consider why it is that Merleau-Ponty asserts so categorically that politics is an order of violence.

Marx believed that violence exists in human relations because there is exploitation and class struggle. For him the question of violence presented few moral or philosphical difficulties: violence would cease with the abolition of classes, but until then it would be inherent in the struggle for human liberation. Merleau-Ponty gives a qualified endorsement to this position, arguing that a stance of non-violence can never amount to more than a tacit endorsement of ruling-class violence (HT xviii). There is thus no moral problem about choosing to use violence *per se*: we cannot avoid doing so. The questions can only concern specifics—the degree of violence we use, against whom and with what effects. But for Merleau-Ponty these questions are both serious and difficult, their difficulty being compounded by the fact that, in his view, class struggle is not the only source of violence. There are other and more extensive causes of violence than class struggle. These are, firstly, the subject-object dichotomy in human relations, which Hegel described in his account of the 'master-slave' dialectic; secondly, and more fundamentally, the role of contingency in our lives.

Merleau-Ponty discusses the 'master-slave' dialectic in the *Phenomenology of Perception* and—as we saw in chapter 2—he refuses to accord it the status of an *a priori* of human existence: there is not an inevitable 'struggle to the death' between consciousnesses. I do not *have to* transform the other into an object, nor he me, since we are both part of one and the same intersubjective world and each can be an extension of the other's consciousness. As Merleau-Ponty expresses it, even the attempt to 'objectify' the other remains—inevitably—a form of communication (PP 361). We are, one might say, 'condemned' to communicate for Merleau-Ponty, in the same way that he says we are 'condemned' to meaning (PP xix).

Even so, when Merleau-Ponty comes to discuss politics and history, not long after the publication of the *Phenomenology of Perception*, he returns to the Hegelian formulation that, 'Each self-consciousness aims at the destruction and death of the other' (1971, p. 232). Even though men are intersubjective existences, creators of a common world, men *do* in fact conduct many of their relationships, as Hegel said, on the basis of struggle and violence. Indeed, they create their common world often almost in spite of themselves. They go beyond struggle, to a kind of intersubjectivity, through struggle (S 212). Even though men cannot but recognise each other through their struggle, the overriding element in history has in fact been struggle and the attempt of men to do violence to each other by reducing each other to objects:

. . . because of the fundamental paradox that man is an indivisible consciousness no one is able to affirm himself except by reducing the others to objects.
What accounts for there being a human history is that man is a being who externalises himself, who needs others and nature to fulfil himself, who individualises himself by appropriating certain goods and thereby enters into conflict with other men (HT 102).

However, because men cannot but recognise themselves in their victims, cannot but create the world of human intersubjectivity through their acts of violence, there is the possibility of going beyond the subject-object dualism and consequent 'master-slave' dialectic in which violence is born. It is this possibility that Marxism pursues, in the attempt to establish a classless and non-exploitative society. The outcome is not, however, assured and meanwhile the 'master-slave' dialectic continues to shape history through the means of violence.

If the 'master-slave' dialectic is a source of violence in history which might in time be eliminated, there is another source of violence which, for Merleau-Ponty, must endure as long as there are men: the existence of contingency in all human action. Contingency is inherent in the human condition because history is not, as we have seen, the unfolding of a pre-determined Reason, but the working out of meaning 'in the intercrossing of those activities by which man organises his relations with nature and with other men' (Pr Phil 50). Since there is an unpredictability in the way individual projects intercross and since the meaning of each project is itself ambiguous, even to its author, the meaning of men's acts always transcending their intentions (PP 169; SNS

65–6), history cannot but be contingent and hence—in Merleau-Ponty's view—violent. This is not, of course, to say that it is wholly contingent, wholly unpredictable. Such tendencies are countered by the 'weight' of history, its 'sedimentation' in 'institutions', as well as by the inherence of meaning in history.

Why, one might ask, however, is contingency a source of violence? Some would, on the contrary, acclaim it as the source of human freedom. For Merleau-Ponty too, contingency is a source of freedom insofar as it precludes any inexorable determinacy shaping human history. But, reciprocally, it implies that irrationality and chaos remain a potential threat to meaning and that we can never make judgements or undertake actions with absolute certainty as to the wisdom of the former or the outcome of the latter. In political action in particular, because it is 'the action of one person upon another and because it is collective action' (HT xxxii), contingency tends to compound itself and thus the potential for violence in this realm is especially great.

By violence Merleau-Ponty means a wider phenomenon than the direct use of physical force against individuals. Such subtle distinctions as, for example, Hannah Arendt makes between violence, power, strength, force and authority (1970, pp. 43–56) do not concern him. Essentially any form of objectification of others is violence, any withdrawal from or denial of intersubjectivity. It is for this reason that he describes colonialism, wage labour and unemployment as forms of violence (HT 103). To treat men as units of labour power, to be deployed, bought, or not bought, is to treat men as objects, as things to be used, and not as men with whom we form one inter-world. The direct use of force on the human body or restraints on movement are more overt and visible forms of violence than unemployment, but the latter is no less violent for that. If physical annihilation is the ultimate form of objectification and hence of violence, we should not forget that the less extreme forms of objectification, particularly economic exploitation, are forms of violence too.

While I think it is useful to describe violence more broadly than as the use of physical force, it seems to me that

Merleau-Ponty's formulation is unsatisfactory. By identifying all objectification with violence, Merleau-Ponty leaves us with no criterion for distinguishing possibly beneficial forms of objectification: the professional impersonalism of a doctor or a teacher, for example, or the decision of a parent to discipline a child for its own good, become in his formulation only milder instances of the violence of the torturer or the killer or the exploiter. The concept of violence threatens to become so broad that it is meaningless.

To return, however, to Merleau-Ponty's account, violence does not arise only from the deliberate and callous treatment of others as objects. *Once* there is objectification and class struggle in our world, we cannot but be involved in it and responsible for violence in one form or another. Hence the paradox that individuals who pursue moral ends—be they the liberal ideals of justice and freedom, or the Marxian goal of a non-exploitative society[1]—cannot avoid violent consequences stemming from their actions.

If all courses of action involve violent consequences, how are we to choose between them? We cannot avoid choosing and deciding, for even inaction is a decision. The sceptic's position, that since the pursuit of all goals leads to violence it does not matter which we pursue, is also unacceptable. Firstly, it is also an implicit acceptance of the violence of the *status quo*. Secondly, by denying the possibility of meaningful choices and morality *a priori*, it precludes them when in fact it might be that they are possible (Pri Per 26). We have then to work on the assumption that, in spite of the inevitability of violence, there *are* significant moral choices to be made and policies to be pursued, even though there can be no certainty that this is the case. Thus, it seems that, ultimately, Merleau-Ponty's argument for the possibility of morality in politics rests on faith—if on a 'good faith', which it is reasonable to believe in (SNS 172–81; SNS 181–7).

It is reasonable to have faith in the possibility of morality not because of God or Universal Mind or the necessary end of History, but because of what men are: because they continually transcend their individual projects and cannot but create and recreate the human world in the process; because they are bodily and perceiving existences, opening on to the same world and inextricably linked in a dialectic both with it and with each other. Just as there can be meaning in history because to be human is to call it forth, there can be morality.

Merleau-Ponty uses the term 'humanism' as a moral as well as a political term. It describes the kind of morality which he thinks is implicit in human existence. He attempts to distinguish his use of the term, from the intellectual and elitist usages he says it has previously had in Western history, as the assertion of the superiority of Western values and culture (HT 176). Humanism, as he means it, starts by recognising that there is violence in human relationships, and the humanist strives, from within the web of violence in which he is caught, to bring about 'man's effective recognition by his fellow men throughout the world' (S 222). This humanism, he says, 'acknowledges in every man a power more precious than his productive capacity . . . as a being capable of self-determination and of situating himself in the world' (HT 176).

'Self-determination'; 'man's effective recognition by his fellow men'. Fine emotive phrases; noble goals to pursue in the face of violence and contingency. But fundamentally, it seems to me, no different as moral goals than say, 'the right to freedom' or the 'right to equal treatment'. They are equally abstract and intangible universal concepts as those of liberalism and equally liable to become the ideological tools of an elite. Merleau-Ponty is lamentably vague about the meaning of these phrases. They are never made 'concrete' and yet they are the criteria in the name of which he criticises 'abstract' liberalism.

The only way in which Merleau-Ponty manages to make his concept of 'humanism' more concrete is to link it to Marxism, at least until the early 1950s. As the 'praxis' of the oppressed, of the proletariat, Marxism alone can hope to transcend violence, to create the society in which men recognise each other and in which their interconnectedness becomes the source not of conflict, but of an autonomy grounded in mutual dependence (SNS 130). Thus it is that the immediate priorities come to be the furthering of the proletarian struggle, although, as we shall see, the paradoxes of violence and morality are revealed in their most acute form in that struggle.

The Unique Role of the Proletariat

Merleau-Ponty admits in *Humanism and Terror* that neither 'capitalism' nor the 'proletariat' now exists as Marx described it (HT 178-9), and yet he still insists that Marxism is unique, superior to all other political movements, and alone has the potential to transcend violence. Why? The short answer is because Marxism is the theory and action of the proletariat—and the proletariat is unique because it alone is a 'universal class'.

The theory of the universal class was developed by Hegel. For him (1967, pp. 197-8), the universal class were the state bureaucrats who, carrying out the interests of the state, the incarnation of Reason, had no particular or sectional interests. Marx, of course, rejected the idea of the rational state with its disinterested servants, but took up and altered the concept of the universal class to mean that class—the proletariat—which embodies universal suffering and 'wrong' and can only free itself by freeing society as a whole from 'wrong' (1970b, pp. 141-2). The account of the proletariat as the universal class come in one of Marx's earlier works (1843) and still bears the somewhat ethereal marks of his contact with Hegelian philosophy. Later he was to flesh it out with more practical reasons as to why the proletariat had to be the class to institute socialism. It always remains of great importance to Marx that the proletariat embodies the most extreme form of oppression and alienation, but its revolutionary potential is seen to be mediated through more concrete processes, such as its physical concentration, brought about by capitalism, which permits the spread of revolutionary ideas and organisation, the tendency of capitalism to increasingly acute crises which politicise the proletariat, etc.

For Merleau-Ponty, on the other hand, it is the simple unmediated universality of the proletariat which makes it a 'privileged' class, the possible vehicle of historical truth and initiator of the era of morality. The universality of the proletariat lies, for Merleau-Ponty, in the fact that it alone experiences dependency—which is a fact for all men in the era of the world market—as total and as total alienation (HT 115). Thus, for the proletariat, 'individuality or self-consciousness and class consciousness are absolutely identical' (HT 115). The proletarian *lives* his universality inescapably since, in his dependency, he cannot achieve consciousness of himelf without consciousness of others. It is for this reason that the proletariat 'is the sole authentic intersubjectivity because it alone lives simultaneously the separation and union of individuals' (HT 116–17).

Why can no other group than the proletariat claim to be the vehicle of progress towards a humanist society? Merleau-Ponty poses the possible refutation of his argument: could one not, he asks, imagine philosophies of history which would bind men's destiny to the wisdom of other groups or individuals? The answer he gives is emphatically negative: '. . . a group of men cannot assume an historical mission—the task of bringing history to an end and creating humanity—unless they are capable of recognising other men as such and being recognised in turn' (HT 154–5). All other groups or important individuals have in history a controlling or coercive role to play which precludes such mutuality. The proletariat alone have a historical role which is not coercive and thus are able to recognise their fellow men, rather than objectifying them; they are the only group which can have relationships of 'reciprocity' with all men. It is from this intrinsic quality that what Merleau-Ponty calls their 'task' or 'historical mission' stems: to create history as the advent of humanity. This conception of the basis of the 'historical mission' of the proletariat is much narrower and more abstract than is Marx's. It concentrates on the proletariat primarily as an ethical entity, the vehicle of the new humanistic order and tends to ignore the concrete role of the proletariat within production. Thus Marx's emphasis on the inherent conflict of interest between capital and the proletariat as a primary source of the dialectic is not to be found in Merleau-Ponty's account of the 'proletarian mission'.

It is possible, of course, Merleau-Ponty points out, that the proletariat will not fulfil its mission. But if it fails, there exists no other group which will be able to take it up. It will mean that, 'the world and our existence are a senseless tumult', even that, 'there is no history—if history means the advent of humanity and humanity the mutual recognition of men as men' (HT 155–6). It is, I think, doubtful whether we do have to identify history with the process of the 'advent of humanity', as Merleau-Ponty states here. For the attempt to interpret it as such directly contradicts the phenomenological conception of history Merleau-Ponty had developed in the *Phenomenology of Perception*. There he had argued that *every* event, *every* phenomenon, must be examined for its own *intrinsic* meaning, and not be reduced to a mere link in some vaster process of the unfolding of history towards a pre-given end (PP xviii–xix).

A further problem of this view of history as the mission of the proletariat—already raised in the previous chapter—is that if, as Merleau-Ponty affirms in the *Phenomenology of Perception*, intersubjectivity and truth are inherent in *all* human existence, there is no reason to insist that the proletariat has to have the special task of developing them. In spite of Merleau-Ponty's identification of Marxism with the 'philosophy of existence', the implication of the '*Phenomenology of Perception* is not the development of humanism through class struggle, but that harmony is a possibility inherent in man qua man, irrespective of class. Yet when he moves more explicitly to the field of politics, and especially in *Humanism and Terror*, Merleau-Ponty firmly links the development of reason and harmony to the ascendancy of the proletariat.

Claude Lefort has argued (1963, p. 30) that 'the bond between logic and contingency' and its implications form the central theme of *Humanism and Terror*. I would agree, for it is this bond which forms the context within which Merleau-Ponty considers proletarian action. The proletariat is not just the class which contains the possibility of *morality*; it is also the carrier of the 'Logos', the potential *rationality* of history. In spite of the arguments in the *Phenomenology of Perception* as to the inherent rationality of all human action, it seems, in *Humanism and Terror* that in this matter the proletariat is—yet again—privileged. Why?

Again the answer lies in the alleged universality of the proletariat. Insofar as truth comes into existence, it is as the unity of individual and general consciousness (PP 448–9). But it is, in Merleau-Ponty's view, the proletariat alone who actually live the unity of individual and general consciousness, since they cannot, in their condition of total alientation and dependency, develop consciousness of self without consciousness of others. It must be stressed that they *live* their consciousness of others. Their recognition of humanity is not purely intellectual, but is implicit in any attempt to overcome their own individual oppression. It is this which is implied in the Marxian notion of 'praxis': consciousness of self, consciousness of others and the attempt to transcend the situation of self and hence, necessarily, of others, are unified in what Merleau-Ponty describes as 'a theory of concrete subjectivity and concrete action' (HT 22), which is Marxist 'praxis'.

Marxism is often accused of being an a-moral theory, but in the notion of proletarian 'praxis' it incorporates its ethics in concrete action. For Marx, there was no fundamental conflict between 'the exigencies of realism and those of ethics' (HT 125), since they are unified in proletarian action. The ethics of the proletariat arise from its situation. The proletariat does not pursue 'ends', through a process of reasoning, from principles, but is 'a force polarised toward certain values by the very logic of the situation it encounters' (HT 127). Those values must, as we have seen, be inherently humanistic. Thus for Marxists, the alternative 'ethics or politics' should never arise. And yet, Merleau-Ponty argues, in the history of Marxism since Marx, 'the dilemma of conscience and politics *has* existed' (HT xxxi).

Marxism, as theory, is a humanism and the proletariat is the only class capable of developing humanism concretely. But Marxism, as Marx developed it, is still a theory, albeit a theory of the concrete. When it becomes action, as in Russia in 1917, it enters the world of contingency and, like any other politics, runs the risk of diversion. Marxist values are humanist, but the attempt to translate them into fact, to engage them in the contingent, ambiguous and violent world of politics, implies their possible subversion into the opposite of humanism—terror.

The question for Merleau-Ponty, as for Sartre (for example, in his play, *Les Mains Sales*), is whether Marxism can transcend the paradox of humanism and terror; whether it can develop a morality which is not subverted by the violence in which it must embroil itself, but is able to transcend that violence, to establish the 'recognition of man by man'. The question is asked from two different aspects: the individual and the general. From the individual viewpoint, Merleau-Ponty asks the very 'existential' question: what sense the individual actor can make of his own actions; whether Marxism and proletarian 'praxis' permit the individual to act morally in spite of—or even through—the use of violent means. From the general viewpoint he asks the (related) question: as a historical movement, is Marxism able to transcend its own use of violence? In answering this question he feels obliged to consider developments in the Soviet Union where, if Marxism is to be more than a dream, violence should be seen to be eliminating itself; or at least there should be seen to be a possibility that it will eliminate itself.

Morality, Violence and the Individual

Hegel, Merleau-Ponty reminds us, 'believed in a Reason beyond the alternatives of interior and exterior which enables man to lead simultaneously a conscious and an empirical life —to be the same for himself as he is for others' (HT 186. The quotation comes from Hegel, 1967, para 118). But Hegel's reign of Reason has not yet come into being; and even if in Marx's proletariat we can find such a unity of consciousness and empirical life as Hegel described, its realm of final harmony is also yet to come. We are still, in Hegel's terms, in the era of abstract Understanding. Marxism strives for a morality beyond either that of intentions or consequences. It claims, in the proletariat, to have found a vehicle for a morality based on human recognition, in which intention and consequence should coincide. But until the realm of final harmony is reached, such a coincidence cannot be assured. Meanwhile, the Marxist must act, but can never be sure that his actions will be morally justifiable: he must commit acts of violence to help bring about the end of violence, but without ever being sure of the outcome of his acts.

I have already discussed Merleau-Ponty's criticism of the ethics which follow from the maxim, 'ignore the consequences of actions'. These are the ethics of Alain and classical liberalism which are ultimately an excuse for not taking responsibility for our actions, since our conscience can remain clear, come what may, as long as we acted from the right principles. Merleau-Ponty also considers and rejects, with Hegel (HT 186), the position that judges actions *only* by their consequences. This position at least has the merit of judging our actions in relation to the world which they affect. But by itself it wholly ignores the question of intentions and the fact that consequences can only be judged in relation to other criteria which we have chosen to start out from. Without reference to other values or intentions, this position can only come to mean that whatever succeeds is good—a position which Merleau-Ponty firmly rejects since it could only be justified if there was, with no shadow of doubt, an Absolute Mind guiding the course of History, while in reality 'we do not *know* the future' (HT xxxv).

Both intentions *and* consequences must be taken into account in judging the morality of political actions. The moral tragedies which can confront the individual arise from the chasm which can however open between intentions and consequences within the contingent world of politics. It is such a fissure between what Merleau-Ponty characterises as the subjective element of an act, the intention, and its objective element, its consequences, which brought about the tragic dilemma of Bukharin, for example. The tragedy arises because, although the consequences of our actions might be very different from our intentions, we are still responsible for the former and cannot disown them:

Historical responsibility transcends the categories of liberal thought—intention and act, circumstance and will, objective and subjective . . . it substitutes for the individual as he feels himself to be a role or phantom in which he cannot recognise himself, but in which he must see himself, since that is what he was for his victims (HT 43).

A somewhat analogous case to that of Bukharin, which Merleau-Ponty discusses, is that of the collaborators during the Nazi occupation of France and their trials after the war. There are, he suggests, certain parallels between the trial of Bukharin and that of Laval and Pétain[2] which cast light on the problem of historical responsibility. Both the trials of the French collaborators and the Moscow trials 'might be seen as the drama of subjective honesty and objective treason' (HT

44). There is no convincing evidence that Laval and Pétain actually plotted to destroy the French army or sold themselves to the Germans, just as there is no clear evidence that Bukharin was involved in Fascist plots against the Soviet Union. Laval and Pétain probably acted from the best of intentions, doing what they thought was in the interests of France, given their assumption that a German victory was assured. But such a victory—as events were to prove—was not assured and thus their actions, instead of being a bowing to the inevitable, were the deliberate *choice* of a policy which made a German victory more likely. It is not simply the case that the collaborators made a mistake and misread history. For in the process, they also *made* history (HT 39). There can be no such thing as neutral or objective judgements in history, for all judgements entail a position and carry a historical weight.

A further interesting parallel which Merleau-Ponty draws between the French and the Russian trials concerns the issue of impartial justice. The possibility of impartial judges and juries implies the existence of disinterested people, outsiders to the case. Such a disinterest might appear possible in times of normality, but in times of revolution, war or occupation, when the 'struggle to the death' which is intrinsic to politics comes to the fore, it is not. Thus, in the French case, the only possibilities for every citizen were collaboration or resistance and society became wholly polarised (HT 41). Since every Frenchman had to choose—even the refusal to choose being an implicit choice for the *status quo*—to expect 'neutral' or impartial justice for the collaborators would be to expect the impossible. The collaborators were found guilty not before an impartial court of justice, but before the court of history. Similarly, in the Moscow trials, the defendants could only be judged in the name of history.

Where, however, the Moscow trials differ from those of the French collaborators is that in the latter case history had already shown the individuals concerned to have been wrong; while in the former, judgement was passed in the name of a still unknown future. Thus in the Moscow trials, because they judged in the name of the future, there was yet another level of uncertainty. What was taking place there was a 'struggle to the death' between different perceptions of the path the revolution—and hence history—*ought* to take (HT 27). It was Stalin's claim that his view of the future was the objective truth which enabled him to justify the Trials and other forms of Terror in its name; yet clearly his view was not the objective truth—any more than was Bukharin's or Trotsky's. It is a mistaken reading of Marxism to think that it can tell one the necessary and 'objective' path to follow, without doubt or ambiguity, and the Trials are witness to this fact. For Marxism, as praxis, *creates* meaning rather than discovering it ready-made; and there is no reason to suppose that individual Marxists will arrive at the identical path or truth to pursue, since each starts from his own situation and perspective, as well as from his place within the proletarian movement (HT 94).

But even when Marxists come to realise—as did Bukharin—that there is no objective and definitive truth that Marxism tells them which could justify their actions, they still have to act on their perception of events—hence to make history and be responsible for what they do. The violence of the revolution does not stem initially from the objectivist and determinist interpretation of Marxism that developed in Russia, but from the realities of the political situation there. From the fact that revolution, as an unmasked form of the 'struggle to the death' and the use of violence against exploiters and oppressors, leaves no neutral middle ground. One is for the revolution or against it; one is comrade or traitor—and yet such judgements have to be made according to the criteria of an unknown future and in the flow of contingent events that can make a non-sense of our decisions.

How then, on this ground of violence and uncertainty can the individual act meaningfully or morally? One might, on Merleau-Ponty's analysis, be tempted to shrug and simply say that the world is inherently irrational, that it is absurd and a-moral, that we are condemned to the existence of indefinite violence and that Marxism can show us no way out of this situation. But to draw such conclusions from Merleau-Ponty's analysis is to ignore his faith in the intrinsic possibility of reason and intersubjectivity in human existence. In *Humanism and Terror*, having described at length the dilemmas of Bukharin and also of Trotsky, he is still at pains to assert that faith, 'the future', he tells us, 'is only probable' and never certain. But that does not mean that it is wholly unshaped or random: 'it is not any empty zone in which we can construct gratuitous projects: it is sketched before us like the beginning of the day's end, and its outline is ourselves' (HT 95).

If individuals were isolated or pure consciousness, then neither truth nor morality would be possible. But since individuals are rooted in one and the same dialectic of objective and subjective factors, there is the possibility that they can participate in the creation of truth—a harmony of perspectives—and morality—'The recognition of man by man'. Taken in isolation, their intentions can be mocked by the force of historical contingency; but as part of a historical process which transcends the individual qua isolated individual consciousness, it is possible that their intentions and actions and their consequences will contribute to the advent of morality and the decline of violence between men. Thus there is no purely personal solution to the moral dilemmas posed for individuals by the political world. It is only if history, through the vehicle of the proletariat, is moving towards the era of morality, that the individual can resolve his own moral problems within that movement.

What we have to know, then, is whether the historical process that is proletarian Marxism *is* in fact moving towards a humanist society; whether the violence of the proletarian movement—and especially of the Soviet Union—'is not the infantile disorder of a new history or merely an episode in an unchanging history' (HT 98).

Morality, Violence and the Proletarian Movement

What led Merleau-Ponty to pose this question and to have such doubts was his perception of events in the Soviet Union and the policies pursued by the French Communist Party. But the question having been raised, Merleau-Ponty attempts an answer to it that goes beyond empirical observation of the Soviet Union. There are, he suggests, certain problems inherent in Marxism that make it quite probable that proletarian violence will not progressively eliminate itself. These problems centre on the nature of the proletariat and its relations to the Party, and on the possible divorce of subjective and objective elements once Marxism passes into action, as revolution guided by a vanguard party.

One of the areas of ambiguity, not to say obscurity, in *Humanism and Terror* is that of the relation between Marxist theory, later Bolshevik theory and the political praxis of the Russian Revolution. It is not clear how far Merleau-Ponty sees the problems as inherent in Marx's theory, or whether they are problems of the Russian Revolution only. At points he suggests that Marxist theory and later communist praxis are quite distinct (see for example, HT 23–4; HT xxi). Yet the way he formulates the problems at other times implies that they do not appertain to the unique set of historical conditions in Russia but are fundamental to the revolutionary enterprise as Marx conceived it and are inherent in *all* revolutionary undertakings.

The fundamental problem of Marxism, which is likely to result in institutionalised violence, stems, Merleau-Ponty thinks, from the fact that the proletariat does not in reality act as it should act according to Marx's theory; it does not, in its behaviour, bear the marks of a universal class and is often very 'backward' in its political consciousness. The Leninist theory of the Party was therefore developed to bridge the gap between the theoretical role of the proletariat and its empirical behaviour. Since the proletariat is often divided and confused, leadership of the revolutionary movement has to be in the hands of those who realise its objective potential—the Party. The task of the Party, in Lenin's view, is to clarify the proletariat to itself and to lead it forward, though 'only one step ahead': to reveal to the proletariat its own will and potential.

It is in the transformation of this theoretical formulation into action that certain kinds of violence are born, says Merleau-Ponty. Merleau-Ponty does not appear to question the theoretical formulation. He seems implicitly to assume that a vanguard party *is* necessary, is part and parcel of Marxian praxis, while also arguing that a possibly unacceptable and undiminishing degree of violence is implicit in its existence—forms of violence over and above those used on the capitalist and allied classes.

It is implied in the theory of the vanguard party that one part of the proletariat (those in the Party) think and will for the rest. Such a formulation, Merleau-Ponty argues, has to involve a kind of force *against* the proletariat:

> Lenin and his comrades did what the masses wanted in the depths of their will and to the extent of their self-awareness; but to act according to someone's deepest convictions, such as one had defined them is precisely to force him, as when a father forbids his son a foolish marriage 'for his own good' (HT 84).

Thus Merleau-Ponty argues, right from the beginning and not only in the Stalinist era, the Revolution was also a dictatorship *over* the proletariat. Acting for the proletariat 'for their own good', the Party implied a form of objectification of the proletariat and thus, in Merleau-Ponty's view, a form of violence against it.

The concept of the Party and its dictatorship also implies what Merleau-Ponty describes as 'the dictatorship of truth', by which he means the dictatorship of what can never be more than a partial and subjective truth. For,

> ... as long as there are men, the future will be open and there will only be a probabilistic calculation and no absolute knowledge. Consequently 'the dictatorship of truth' will always be the dictatorship of a group, and to those who do not share in it, it will appear purely arbitrary (HT 92).

Revolution is, of necessity, the imposition of the subjective perceptions of the leadership on the rank-and-file of the Party and on the proletariat; and Marxist theory, whether or not it claims objective truth, cannot avoid the imposition of the subjective decisions of the few on the many. The problem is inherent in the transformation of theory into action. For no general theory, such as Marxism, can provide the full basis on which we can plan *specific* actions.

Lenin himself recognised this, Merleau-Ponty says, when he wrote that the general principles of communism must be applied '*to the specific features* in the objective development towards communism which are different in each country and which we must be able to discover, study and predict' (cited HT 118). Such applications, Merleau-Ponty asserts, must be made on the basis of the individual perceptions and judgements of the top Party cadres and they always run the risk of becoming detached from the will of the proletariat, in whose interests they are supposed to be made. The subjective and the objective elements of history, which Marxian praxis claims to unify in the vehicle of the proletariat, threaten to become divorced and the subjective will of the Party leadership to dominate the revolutionary process.

According to the Leninist theory, of course, the leaders' perceptions should not diverge radically from those of the masses. The perceptions of both leaders and led arise within the process of interaction of the vanguard and the mass and within the context of their common struggle against the forces of capitalism. However, Merleau-Ponty is surely correct in saying that the perceptions of the leadership diverged radically from those of the masses in Russia, certainly under Stalin and probably earlier, and that this divergence points to the need to question the Leninist theory of the Party. I would, however, criticise Merleau-Ponty for not probing further: *theoretical* problems about the Party will not suffice to explain Stalinism. The question why such a wide gulf developed between leaders and led in Russia cannot be adequately answered only at the level of theory—nor of course simply on the basis of conflicting economic interest of different strata. If ever Merleau-Ponty was actually going to apply his phenomenological method to the study of historical phenomena, it should have been to this question: what were the different life experiences, what the different ways of being and perceiving that gave rise to the emergence of such divergences of political consciousness within the Party and the masses in Russia? That Merleau-Ponty fails to pose such a question and limits his discussion to the question of Leninist theory indicates a certain lack of interest in the concrete application of phenomenological method, a lack of interest which I have already noted in relation to his critique of liberalism.

What are the consequences of the divorce between the Party leadership and the will and consciousness of the proletariat? Above all, the Revolution becomes a voluntaristic enterprise, the will of a few men attempting to force history. At this point, there cease to be clear limits to the use of violence. The door is open to opportunism, to detours and compromises which can threaten to turn Marxist humanism into its opposite, the permanent institutionalisation of violence: 'Nothing allows us to say precisely: here Marxist politics end and there the counter-revolution begins' (HT 91). Hence the boundary between revolutionary violence, which should be self-eliminating, and ordinary political violence disappears.

Similarly, once the revolutionary enterprise becomes separated from the proletariat, it runs the risk of losing its direction or meaning. The shifts, the adaptations to contingent events, the switches in policy, cease to be part of a revolutionary development and become no more than the subjective will of a group of leaders. Like the line between revolutionary and non-revolutionary violence, the line between detours and compromises which are still Marxist and those which have ceased to be so is not clear-cut: '. . . there comes a time when a detour ceases to be a detour, when the dialectic is no longer a dialectic and we enter a new order of history which has nothing in common with Marx's philosophy of the proletariat' (HT 150). Thus the question, as Merleau-Ponty poses it, is whether, at the end of the tortuous road from War Communism, to NEP, to Stalinist Terror, there is any Marxism left in the politics of the Soviet Union and whether, therefore, there is still any possibility of the progressive elimination of violence there.

Merleau-Ponty's answer is in the negative. What has happened in Russia is a process in which the 'objective' factors of the economic base have (at the 'subjective' decision of the leadership), been over-emphasised at the expense of the most important 'subjective' factor, mass revolutionary consciousness. As a result, the Revolution has ceased to be a dialectical process and has substituted the voluntaristic actions of the leadership for the consciousness of the proletariat (HT 135). Thus the possibilities for humanism and truth, intrinsic to the proletariat, have become lost to the Revolution and a society has emerged in which both terror and inequality have been institutionalised (HT 138–9).

One might expect that at the end of his investigations Merleau-Ponty would conclude that morality in the world of politics is impossible and that the orders of truth and violence are destined to remain forever discrete. But Merleau-Ponty refuses to accept such pessimism and attempts instead to rescue Marxism from the monstrosity it appears to have engendered. He uses two different arguments, both of which ultimately imply little more than the need for faith—albeit 'reasonable faith'—the need not to close the door definitively on the possibility of truth and morality developing by saying they are impossible.

The first argument is that, in spite of its present abandonment in Russia, the proletariat is not dead. It is too early to say that Marxism has been disproved, for every so often the proletariat again threatens to intervene in history. The fact that governments so fear the proletariat is one proof of its continuing potential power (HT 158). In France, working-class opposition to the German occupation gave another proof of the tenacity of the proletariat. The class struggle might be 'masked' and the class divisions ambiguous much of the time, but both still exist and a resurgence of proletarian activity might still bring about the vindication of Marxism. A corollary to this argument is, says Merleau-Ponty, that the Communist Party, in spite of all its compromises and duplicities, still has a revolutionary potential and is entitled to a measured 'critical support' for as long as it has the adherence of the proletariat—which it still does (HT 160).

Merleau-Ponty's second argument for continuing to have faith in Marxism is that there is no other alternative. To admit that Marxism has been proved wrong is to admit that violence and chaos are the timeless lot of men, that there is ultimately no meaning in history:

Marxism is not just any hypothesis that might be replaced tomorrow by some other. It is the simple statement of those conditions without which there would be neither any humanism, in the sense of a mutual relation between men, nor any rationality in history (HT 153).

But even if it is the only possible philosophy of history, the point might come where we have to reject Marxism. The question is, how long can one wait, giving Marxism the benefit of the doubt, to see if history shapes to its theory? Or, conversely, at what point does one decide that the detours have ceased to be detours and have, on a world scale, become something wholly other than proletarian Marxism? The decision cannot be made according to the guidelines of theory. For what such a decision involves is testing theory against concrete reality, as one perceives it. It involves making one of those uncertain and anguished choices which Merleau-Ponty sees as unavoidable in the world of politics and history. In 1947, and for several years afterwards, Merleau-Ponty was not yet ready to make such a decision. He continued to call for faith and to maintain, in the pages of *Les Temps Modernes*, a policy of 'critical support' and 'wait and see Marxism'.

Notes

1 I realise that many Marxists would object to the description of the non-exploitative society as the moral end of Marxism. Marxism, they would say, is a science and has nothing to do with morals. However, it seems to me that, its scientific claims notwithstanding, Marxism is, in fact an intensely moral theory; communism is not only what its science tells it *will* happen, it is also what *ought* to happen, a moral imperative. (See Kamenka, 1962 and Mészáros, 1970, especially Ch. VI).
2 Pierre Laval (1883–1945), headed the 'Vichy' government, in the Southern part of France in 1942. He was tried and executed for collaboration in 1945. Philippe Pétain (1856–1951), was France's foremost military hero from World War One. However, he agreed to become 'Head of State' during the German occupation, from 1940–1944. He was also condemned to death in 1945, but his sentence was reduced to life imprisonment.

PART 3:

RETREAT

6 The Rejection of Marxist Politics

The 'Conversion'

THE Korean War broke out in the summer of 1950 and Merleau-Ponty's position of 'critical support' for communism came to an abrupt end. Sartre recalls that in the summer of 1950 the events were unclear from France (1965, pp. 191–2). Information was lacking on the background to the conflict and on USA connivance in its beginning—'The only established fact was that the Northern troops had been the first to cross the dividing parallel'. The communist press, however, persisted in claiming the opposite. To Merleau-Ponty, Korea appeared as a sudden and irrefutable proof that the Soviet Union considered war with the USA and its allies inevitable and that, to pre-empt it, Stalin was willing to commit acts of aggressive imperialism which demonstrated that the possibility of a return to a humanist Marxism no longer existed in Russia.

The general political atmosphere in France at the time was one of paranoia. There was widespread anxiety that if the conflict escalated the Soviet Union would invade Western Europe. A third World War was seen by many, including Merleau-Ponty, as a real possibility, with Europe as the main battleground. Within this context, a position of 'critical support' became untenable in Merleau-Ponty's view. It was not, Sartre says, that he 'took sides with the other monster, capitalist imperialism', but that suddenly the Soviet Union was as bad: a Soviet occupying force in France would be an imperialist occupation, not a socialist liberation. If that was the probable outcome of Soviet policy, 'critical support' changed its meaning and became an endorsement of Soviet imperialism which Merleau-Ponty was not willing to make.

Sartre describes Merleau-Ponty's change of opinion as a 'conversion' (1965, p. 198). Korea was the 'instant' that showed Merleau-Ponty 'the horror of Stalinism', when the revelations about the labour camps and such foreign policy manoeuvres as the Berlin Blockade had not previously forced him to give up his position of 'critical support'. Sartre's description is apt, for it would indeed seem to have been a sudden shift of perception on Merleau-Ponty's part rather than any fundamental alteration in Soviet policy which occasioned his changed position.

Merleau-Ponty's response to Korea, says Sartre, was silence. If one could no longer give even 'critical support' to the Soviet Union and one could not condone imperialist capitalism either and there was no neutral ground left between them, then there was simply nothing left to say. Sartre quotes the following conversation between Merleau-Ponty and himself:

'The only thing left for us is silence'.
'Who is "us"?' I said, pretending not to understand.
'Well, us, *Les Temps Modernes*'.
'You mean, you want us to put the key under the door?'
'No, not that. But I don't want us to breathe another word of politics'.
'But why not?'
'They're fighting'.
'Well, all right, in Korea'.
'Tomorrow they'll be fighting everywhere'.
'And even if they were fighting here, why should we be quiet?'
'Because brute force will decide the outcome. Why speak to what has no ears?'

(1965, p. 189)

Sartre, somewhat resentfully, went along with Merleau-Ponty's demands for silence. *Les Temps Modernes* produced no editorial comment on Korea and generally underplayed politics. Although Merleau-Ponty resigned from his post as political editor, he remained 'editor-in-chief' of the journal until 1952, during which period he wrote nothing for the journal on politics and to some extent imposed his silence on the rest of the team. Meanwhile Sartre, confronted by the same problem of a world divided in two, underwent his own 'conversion', precipitated by the 'Duclos Affair' (the arrest and frame-up of a leading French communist on the eve of anti-American demonstrations in Paris in June 1952), into a position of whole-hearted support for the Communist Party. The two men were thus moving in opposite directions and, in Sartre's view, were already engaged in what he describes as a 'labour of rupture' (1965, p. 205) when Merleau-Ponty's resignation from *Les Temps Modernes*, precipitated by a conflict about an editorial matter, abruptly ended their relationship for several years.

Between 1950 and 1954, Merleau-Ponty published virtually nothing on politics. Indeed, he published very little in that period altogether and, from Sartre's account, appeared very little in public. From what little Merleau-Ponty did say or publish in this period, it would appear that the 'conversion' against the Soviet system at the time of Korea was not yet a wholehearted conversion away from Marxism.[1] The latter, according to Lefort (1974, p. xiii), was to take place only after an intensive re-reading of Marxist literature, starting in 1952, from which Merleau-Ponty was to conclude that the roots of the Bolshevik aberrations were already to be found in the writings of Marx. This conclusion was to be formulated in *Adventures of the Dialectic*, written mainly between April and December 1954 and published in 1955.

Adventures of the Dialectic is a puzzling book. Its purpose would appear to have been to justify Merleau-Ponty's decision to end his support for Marxist politics of any kind and to announce his move towards the kind of radical, or 'new', liberalism which he outlines in the 'Epilogue'. However, the book does not proceed, as one might have expected it would, by any systematic refutation of his earlier defence of Marxism and critique of liberalism—or indeed by any kind of systematic argument. Instead, it consists of what Merleau-Ponty himself describes as 'several small works' (AD 3), sandwiched together between a Preface and an Epilogue in which he attempts (not very successfully), to tie them together. The 'small works', best described as essays, are five in number and are concerned, in order of appearance, one with Weber, one with Lukacs, two with the Russian Bolshevik experience, as theory and as practice, and one with Sartre's Marxism. They purport to show the apparently inevitable collapse of the Marxian dialectic into either objectivism (Lukacs, Lenin and Trotsky) or subjectivism (Sartre).

The main function of the first two essays appears to be to establish a yardstick by which to judge Marxism—and find it wanting. Merleau-Ponty describes Weber's liberalism as self-questioning and 'heroic' (AD 26), since it admits the problem of violence and contingency in politics and, unlike classical liberalism, accepts that although the liberal ideals of truth and freedom are to be struggled for they are not necessarily to be attained (AD 25-8). Lukacs, who was once a student of Weber's, integrates the self-questioning implicit in Weber's viewpoint into Marxism in his early, humanistic work. In the work of these two men, Merleau-Ponty purports to find the criteria (in a rather loose sense of the word) by which Marxism can be judged a failure and thus also to provide, in some unspecified way, a justification for his own return to liberalism. However, the critique of Marxism in the rest of the book is not rigorously tied to these criteria and it is never clearly shown why a return to liberalism is the necessary outcome of the critique of the various Marxisms described. The book as a whole remains incoherent and unsatisfactory, a weak case for the abandonment of Marxism and a still weaker one for the advocacy of liberalism as the alternative.

The Failure of Marxist Theory

Lukacs did not manage to sustain the humanistic and dialectical Marxism of his youth. He made his self-criticism and deferred to the 'naive realism' of Lenin's philosophy—a realism which placed the dialectic in 'objective' matter, made truth supra-historical and turned Marx's materialism into a 'materialist metaphysic' (AD 65). Lenin's theoretical formulations in his main work of philosophy, *Materialism and Empiriocriticism*, make man the object of history and no longer its subject: 'By joining the dialectic with materialist metaphysics', Lenin 'preserves the dialectic but embalms it outside ourselves, in an external reality' (AD 65).

Why did Lenin so alter Marxism and why did Lukacs bow to his theory and agree to criticise his own work? The answers to these two questions are to be found, Merleau-Ponty thinks, in an examination of the works of Marx. The 'discordancy between naive realism and dialectical inspiration' (AD 62), which is the essence of the dispute between

Lenin and the 'young' Lukacs, is already to be found within the works of Marx. It was only until 1850 that Marx wished to 'realise' philosophy in a 'concrete' dialectic. After that his emphasis was increasingly on 'scientific socialism' and the dialectic became 'the simple verification of certain descriptive features of history, even of nature' (AD 62).

This assertion, that the basis of Lenin's metaphysical materialism and scientism is to be found in Marx's work, is central to Merleau-Ponty's argument. For it is this which justifies, in his eyes, rejecting not just the Soviet version of Marxism but *all* Marxism: 'there is not much sense trying Bolshevism all over again at the moment when its revolutionary failure becomes apparent. But neither is there much sense in trying Marx all over again if his philosophy is involved in this failure' (AD 91). Considering, however, how central this argument is to Merleau-Ponty's new position, it is not one that he devotes much space to, or defends very convincingly.

In an earlier work (see SNS 128), Merleau-Ponty had already pointed to the shift between Marx's earlier and later writings, but had concluded that the scientism of the later works was no more than a veneer introduced for polemical reasons and which did not deviate from the basic thrust of Marx's earlier works. Merleau-Ponty does not, however, now attempt to refute this earlier interpretation. Instead, he ignores it, while providing very little evidence to support his new interpretation of Marx. On the contrary, most of the passages where Merleau-Ponty attacks Marx are assertion, unsupported by evidence from the writings of Marx, or, more often, draw on Engels, Lenin or Trotsky for surrogate evidence of what Marx is supposed to have said.

Merleau-Ponty does, however, attempt to back up his new interpretation of Marx with an explanation: if Marx rejected his early dialectical philosophy for a naturalism or metaphysical materialism and if Lukacs had to withdraw his in the face of Lenin's even more objectivist theory, there must be a reason for this; there must be a problem within dialectical philosophy. Merleau-Ponty draws on Korsch's work (see 1972, pp. 50–9), to suggest that 'dialectical and philosophical Marxism' is suited to revolutionary epochs while scientism predominates in stable epochs. The reason for this is, says

Merleau-Ponty, that the dialectical theory of the 'young' Marx and the 'young' Lukacs, lacked a way of conceptualising the weight of history, the 'intertia of infra-structures' (AD 64) adequately. It lacked a conceptualisation of history as neither spirit nor matter, as developing neither according to eternal ideas, nor according to causal laws.

This explanation is, yet again, in direct contradiction with Merleau-Ponty's earlier account of Marxism, although he in no way acknowledges the fact. In the earlier works, Marxism is praised for having *found* such a conceptualisation of history, for providing, in historical materialism, an account of human existence and coexistence in all its dimensions. But now, suddenly, Merleau-Ponty announces that Marxism fails at exactly that point where he had previously argued it is strongest. Furthermore, he explains its failure wholly in intellectual terms, without regard to concrete historical conditions or 'praxis'—in short, non-phenomenologically.

Even if one were to accept this new view of Marxism, the implications that Merleau-Ponty draws from it do not necessarily follow. Were it true that dialectical Marxism does not have an adequate conceptualisation of the historical process, the implications need be neither that it should be abandoned for a metaphysical materialism, as it is implied that the Bolsheviks and Lukacs did, nor that it should be rejected in favour of a vague and idealistic liberalism. If what dialectical Marxism has to offer is as fruitful as Merleau-Ponty had suggested, then another possibility would be to attempt—as he claims to have started doing ten years earlier in the *Phenomenology of Perception*—to deepen and widen its concepts so that they become adequate. Thus, it should be clear, Merleau-Ponty's decision to reject Marxism is not a consequence of his analysis of it: the analysis is a justification of a choice made prior to this examination.

Having argued—or rather asserted—that the tension between the theory of Lenin and that of the 'young' Lukacs is already present in the thought of Marx, Merleau-Ponty then goes on to show that this tension is never resolved within Lukacs' career. The life of Lukacs is a cautionary tale, a symbol for Merleau-Ponty of the inevitably contradictory positions Marxist theoreticians must fall into. On the one hand Lukacs accepted Lenin's realism, with its implications that individual judgement is suspect and the Party the only vehicle of truth. But on the other hand, Lukacs could never accept all the implications of this position. In his theory of literature he still maintained a dialectical position, arguing that literature always expresses something wider than class interest and that, as Merleau-Ponty puts it, 'consciousness may well be false or falsified but . . . there is never a fundamental falsity of consciousness' (AD 68). Lukacs' political writings and adherence and his work on literature remain, says Merleau-Ponty, permanently in contradiction. His defence of 'bourgeois' literature was correctly seen by orthodox communist critics to imply the existence of a certain autonomy from the class struggle in literature, and hence the possibility of a truth beyond class interests.

It is true that Lukacs had a tortured and contradictory career. But a cautionary tale should not be confused with an argument. It seems to me that Lukacs' turns and compromises are probably to be explained more in terms of his desire to remain efficacious within the communist movement than in terms of inevitable internal contradictions of Marxist philosophy. It will not do—and shows yet again an idealism that belies Merleau-Ponty's claim to phenomenological method —to examine the life-work of an individual without taking into account his relations to the men and movements, as well as to the philosophical debates, of his time.

The Dialectic in Action

The inadequacy of the dialectic, according to Merleau-Ponty, exists not only at the level of theoretical formulations, as illustrated by the work of Lenin and Lukacs. It is also (his account of Lukacs' life notwithstanding), apparent in practical politics. Merleau-Ponty takes the political career of Trotsky to exemplify the problems of the dialectic 'in action'. If Trotsky 'did not accomplish the revolutionary resolution of antinomies in practice, it is because he encountered an obstacle there, the same obstacle that Lenin's "philosophy" confusedly attempted to take into account' (AD 74).

The problem of translating theory into action is one which Merleau-Ponty had already considered in *Humanism and*

Terror, where he had made the important points that contingency can deflect actions from the initial intentions behind them and that general principles or policies cannot tell us what to do in specific cases, and that these limitations apply to the Marxist as much as to any other political actor (HT 93–4). But when in *Adventures of the Dialectic* Merleau-Ponty comes to consider Trotsky's failures, these general difficulties are ignored and the blame laid exclusively at the door of Bolshevik and Marxist *theory*. In addition, Marxism and Bolshevism are assumed to be synonymous in much of the account, an assumption which Merleau-Ponty had been at pains to refute in his earlier accounts of Marxism and which now adds to the general confusion and weakness of his argument.

Trotsky's theoretical writings reveal a good understanding of dialectical method, in Merleau-Ponty's view. The source of the dialectic for Trotsky is to be found in the relationship between the masses and the Party: 'In the absence of any metaphysic of history, the dialectic of the proletariat and the Party gathers all others and bears them within itself' (AD 78). Within the dialectic of proletariat and Party the question of ends and means is resolved, the subjective and objective, theory and action are unified and the meaning of history emerges. When, however, Trotsky moved from the realm of theory to that of practical politics, he failed to build on the dialectic of mass and Party because, according to Merleau-Ponty, the categories of Marxist thought themselves precluded his doing so.

The practical politics to which Merleau-Ponty is referring is the power struggle from 1923–1927 in which Trotsky was defeated by Stalin. If Trotsky was sure that his position was correct, one surely would have expected him to carry it to the masses, to argue his case outside the inner circles of the Party. Yet he did no such thing, denying instead that there was any 'programmatic difference' between the Left Opposition and the mainstream of the Party and condoning the suppression of Lenin's 'testament'.[2] Why was this?

Merleau-Ponty's answer is that Trotsky held back from the dialectical course of action because he was blind as to what was happening. And he was blind because what was happening could not be envisioned within the Marxist perspective. For what was happening was the separation of elements that not only later Marxists, but Marx himself, had regarded as inextricably linked—namely, collectivisation and the power of the proletariat. The 'materialistic dialectic', Merleau-Ponty writes:

> *does not separate* collectivisation and planning from the power of the proletariat, *it does not wish to choose* between them, *it does not allow* us to imagine them in conflict. But precisely because the dialectic does not separate them, because Marx never conceived of a collective and planned economy which was not for the benefit of the proletariat . . . it leaves the Marxists without a criterion when they are faced with a regime which separates the two elements of socialism (AD 83–4).

While it is true that Marx does not consider the possibility of a collective and planned economy which is not for the benefit of the proletariat, this does not mean that the possibility is a priori excluded from Marxist analysis, as Merleau-Ponty seems to believe: one surely need not conclude that when Trotsky himself arrived at his analysis of 'Thermidor' and did finally confront what had happened in Russia, that he had to abandon Marxist concepts and categories to do so (see Trotsky, 1945; also Cliff, 1964 and Djilas, 1966, for other Marxist critiques of the Russian Revolution).

Merleau-Ponty believes that the basis of this conceptual inadequacy which he wishes to attribute to Marxism is to be found in what he takes to be the Marxist theory of the Party. It is because the Party and the proletariat are the expression of each other that Marxism cannot conceive of the Party seizing power *from* the proletariat and pursuing policies no longer in the interest of the proletariat. Indeed, if the Party and the proletariat are separated, the truth of history, as Marxism conceives it, is lost. Trotsky, he says, 'hesitated to situate truth outside the Party because Marxism had taught him that truth could not in principle reside anywhere but at the point where the proletariat and the organisation which embodies it are joined' (AD 82–3).

But is the theory of the Party as vital to Marxism as Merleau-Ponty's account assumes? I would suggest that it is not, especially if, unlike Merleau-Ponty, we separate Marx's own ideas from those of the Bolsheviks. In *Humanism and*

Terror, where Merleau-Ponty himself was at pains not to confuse Marxism and Bolshevism, he had emphasised that the *proletariat* is the central concept of Marxism. He had raised the possibility that the Party, which was supposed to embody the proletariat, could displace it and thus distort the revolution (HT 83–4). But in 1947 he did not see that possibility as threatening to falsify the *whole* Marxian analysis, or as negating the proletarian mission irrevocably. It is, I suggest, only by reading Lenin back into Marx—and a rather contentious reading of Lenin at that—that Merleau-Ponty manages to 'prove' that the Marxian dialectic cannot be sustained and is doomed to failure.

Lenin developed his theory of the professional vanguard party not only in response to specifically Russian conditions but also on the basis of a wider assumption about the general incapacity of the proletariat to move from reformist to revolutionary struggle without outside leadership (1960, pp. 144–9 and pp. 216–18). However, as Merleau-Ponty admits, the need for leadership did not imply, in Lenin's formulation, manipulation or coercion of the proletariat, but a dialectical relationship between leader and led, the former never being more than 'a step ahead' of the masses (AD 128). The problem, as Merleau-Ponty sees it, is that this dialectical formulation of the relations between the masses and party—a formulation which is also Trotsky's—is very fine in theory but cannot be sustained in action. The dialectic comes apart: the Party, as the repository of theory, claims that it alone has the truth, in the name of which it feels justified in directing and manipulating the recalcitrant masses, if necessary through terror.

While Merleau-Ponty's account provides a good description of what actually *happened* in Russia under Stalin, there are several difficulties with it as an argument for the total abandonment of Marxism. For Merleau-Ponty is making two questionable assumptions: (1) that Stalinism *had to be* the consequence of implementing the theory; (2) that this theory is absolutely central to Marxism, so that if we have to reject it, we have also to reject Marxism.

Merleau-Ponty is quite explicit about the first of these assumptions, but his argument for it is unconvincing since it is based on a rather dubious psychological concept of 'vertigo' or 'frenzy'. The Bolshevik leader, he says, having read *Capital* and understood Marxist theory, believes himself to know what is true and thus believes that the proletariat *must* be mistaken if it does not agree with him; hence violence becomes justified even against the proletariat, on the grounds that 'Those who will be shot *would understand* tomorrow that they did not die in vain'; the only problem is, Merleau-Ponty adds, 'that they will not be there to understand it' (AD 130). Lenin, Merleau-Ponty says, certainly did not intend such consequences when he developed his theory of leadership, but they are its inevitable outcome.

It seems to me to be nonsense to regard this as the necessary outcome of Lenin's theory. Indeed, even in Merleau-Ponty's account it appears to be more an outcome of human psychology, of the fact that leaders enter a 'state of frenzy' and end up by *abandoning* the theory: 'The assurance of being the carrier of truth is vertiginous' (AD 129). The leader, sure that he knows the truth, becomes over-confident; he abandons Lenin's theory and forces the proletariat along the 'right' path, destroying the dialectical interplay of leaders and mass that was so vital in Lenin's view. In effect, Merleau-Ponty produces a variation of the old adage that 'power corrupts': power and a belief that one has the truth make men frenzied. Such an adage, even if it contains, like most adages, a grain of truth, can hardly provide the grounds for rejecting Marxism which, on Merleau-Ponty's own previous admission, goes further than any other theory in coming to terms with the irrational and violent. The explanation for Stalinism can hardly be as simple as that Stalin was seized with a kind of vertigo which leaders are liable to catch.

The second, and even more fundamental, question which needs considering is whether the Leninist theory of the party really *is* the vital element of Marxism that Merleau-Ponty assumes it to be. Certainly for several decades now, the Communist Party faithful have linked the theories of Marx and Lenin together and called themselves adherents of 'Marxism-Leninism', as if the two were wholly indivisible. Yet Lenin did not, as is often said, simply update Marxism for the twentieth century. He also made significant alterations to it—of which his theory of the Party is perhaps the most fundamental. Merleau-Ponty had earlier been at pains to distinguish Marxism from Bolshevism. But in *Adventures of the Dialectic* he treats them as synonymous. He thus ends up, like the orthodox communists, in the thoroughly a-historical position of ascribing to Marx a theory that grew out of the concrete conditions of the twentieth century and which is not to be encountered in Marx's work.[3]

Today it is a fairly commonplace idea that to be a Marxist need not imply being a Leninist, that a different type of organisation than the vanguard party might be essential for revolution, at least in the advanced capitalist countries. Especially since the events in France of 1968, it has become a commonplace among some sections of the Left, without rejecting Marxism, to stress the need for spontaneous grass-roots action, for workers' self-management, for a fight on the cultural and 'life-style' front, as well as, or even more importantly than, on the economic front. Such ideas did not emerge out of thin air in France in 1968 and already in the early 1950s vanguardism was being questioned in some Marxist circles. Most important of these was a group around the journal, *Socialisme ou Barbarie?*, which included Claude Lefort whom Merleau-Ponty knew well.[4] As early as 1952 Lefort was already arguing that it is impossible to bring consciousness to the workers from without and that all party organisations are inevitably centralising and impede the development of the mass consciousness on which alone a revolution can be based (see Lefort 1952).

It is clear that Merleau-Ponty must have encountered these ideas, but he appears to have ignored them. They are never mentioned in his work, not even to be criticised or rejected. He seems, from the early 1950s, to have wanted nothing to do with the debates within Marxism. Why was this? It is hard to explain. It seems to me that we are forced back to Sartre's idea of a 'conversion': it seems that once Merleau-Ponty had made up his mind, he wanted no further discussion, no blurring of the issues, no shades of grey between the black and white alternatives. Marxism was a proven failure—end of argument. For the 'philosopher of ambiguity' (de Waelhens, 1951) it was a strangely rigid position to take. In the last years of his life Merleau-Ponty was to become again a little less rigid about the failure of Marxism, but in the mid-1950s, and especially in *Adventures of the*

Dialectic, the condemnation is total and unequivocal.

The same rigidity is apparent in another line of attack Merleau-Ponty uses against Marxism in *Adventures of the Dialectic* (pp. 88–90; p. 207). In a rather convoluted neo-Hegelian argument, he accuses Marxism of placing all the 'negativity' and all the 'meaning' of history in the hands of the proletariat. The result, he says, is that after the revolution the proletariat establishes itself in power as pure 'positivity', thereby rupturing the dialectic and instituting the reign of terror:

> . . . precisely because it succeeded and ended up as an institution, the historical movement is no longer itself: it 'betrays' and 'disfigures' itself in accomplishing itself. Revolutions are true as movements and false as regimes (AD 207).

What is obscure about this argument is the authorship of the idea of revolution as negativity. Is it Marx or Merleau-Ponty who 'concentrates all the negativity and all the meaning of history' in the proletariat? Merleau-Ponty had earlier argued against Hegel (and was also to argue against Sartre) that it is an error to postulate a duality between being (positivity) and consciousness (negativity), or to expect the resolution of such a duality in an end to history. He had contrasted Marx to Hegel as the philosopher who overcame this dualism and developed a fully human concept of the dialectic, in which the 'motivating force' was not the proletariat qua economic interest, but the proletariat as an expression of humanity (SNS 129–30). Now, suddenly and without any evidence produced, it appears that Marx is as dualistic as the late Hegel. Additionally, it seems to me, Merleau-Ponty *himself* is arguing—contrary to his general theory of history—that history is a process of wholly polarised negativity and positivity, rather than the process of their interplay. To say that it is inevitable that *all* revolutions, as pure negativities, become pure positivities that wholly suppress the process of negation is to postulate a rigid dualism in history.

A more interesting topic which Merleau-Ponty raises—but unfortunately does not discuss in any real depth—concerns the occurrence of revolution in 'backward' countries. Marx had conceived of the revolution as the culmination of a long, slow process of maturation of the proletariat in the developed capitalist countries. But the first revolution took place in backward Russia and was explained—because it had to be explicable within a Marxist framework—by the addition to Marxist theory, *post hoc*, of the 'law of unequal development'. Perhaps, Merleau-Ponty suggests, it is not so simple. Firstly, it was maybe not an 'accident' that the revolution took place in a backward country; perhaps (unfortunately Merleau-Ponty does not explain why), the proletarian revolution is 'essentially linked to the structure of backward countries' (AD 91–2) and not to advanced capitalism. Secondly, if this is the case, then the humanistic possibilities of Marxism are called into question. For a revolution in a backward country, without a mature proletariat, cannot avoid being such a violent rupture with the past that it must detroy its own intentions, as happened in Russia (AD 92–3). Given the histories of other revolutions since that in Russia—China, Cuba, Vietnam, Mozambique, etc—these are interesting and important questions that Merleau-Ponty raises. But he raises them and purports to answer them only at the level of theory—and at the level of a very schematic theory at that.

One finds here the source of the main weakness of Merleau-Ponty's critique of Marxism. It is his failure to examine the *concrete* conditions of the Russian Revolution. The major thrust of his analysis is an explanation of the ills of the Revolution almost wholly in ideological terms. It is because the *theory*, the ideas, were wrong, that the Revolution degenerated. But as he himself had argued in his attacks on idealist philosophy and liberal idealism, we cannot understand societies only in terms of their ideas. Ideas alone do not make history—not even Marxist ideas. The attempt, in *Adventures of the Dialectic*, to account for the phenomenon of Stalinism almost exclusively by a search for its intellectual origins in and evolution from the writings of Marx, a century before, is not compatible either with Merleau-Ponty's critique of idealism or his advocacy of phenomenological method.

Furthermore, there is in Merleau-Ponty's analysis a kind of fatalism or determinism which conflicts with the fundamental premises of his 'philosophy of existence'. The belief that the degeneration of Marxism was inevitable, that the roots of Stalinism are to be found in the works of Marx himself, implies that the human project is not 'open' and indeterminate, that contingency does not have a significant role to play in history and that, after all, events are shaped by an inexorable logic or causality: the humanistic 'young' Marxs *had to* become a positivist; Leninism *had to* develop into Stalinism.

Sartre's Subjectivism

Having, he believes, shown how Bolshevism destroys the dialectic through its dissolution into objectivism, Merleau-Ponty turns in the last main essay of *Adventures of the Dialectic* to Sartre's work to show its complementary dissolution into subjectivism (AD 97–8). But attractive though this scheme might be, the fact that the Marxian dialectic has been dissolved on different occasions into both objectivism and subjectivism does not demonstrate the need to write it off entirely for the future, or prove that it is doomed to dissolution. Furthermore, one has to question the appropriateness of examining Sartre's work, and in particular his book, *The Communists and Peace* (1969), as a significant proof of the tendency of the dialectic to be destroyed by subjectivism. For Sartre's influence on Marxism, outside a small circle of French intellectuals, was still comparatively small in the early 1950s. Additionally, the book in question was hastily written, is highly polemical and is certainly not one of Sartre's major or best works, or one on which his contribution to Marxism should be uniquely assessed.

The main charges that Merleau-Ponty makes against Sartre are as follows. Fundamental to Sartre's ontology is the distinction between consciousness and things, between nothingness and being (AD 142), a distinction which in the human world becomes that between Self and Other. From this distinction, which Merleau-Ponty had repeatedly argued was groundless, stem various consequences which colour Sartre's political views. By opposing consciousness to matter, Sartre is obliged to view history as the outcome of pure consciousness, or will, and not, as Marx did, as 'a mixed milieu, neither things nor persons' (AD 124)[5]. For Marx (Merleau-Ponty here returns to the 'young' Marx, not the Marx who has been the villain of the former two essays), fact and meaning are always mixed and consciousness situated. But for Sartre, 'conscious awareness is absolute. It gives meaning; and in the case of an event, the meaning it gives is irrevocable' (AD 115). Within this framework, the Revolution and the creation of communism have to be seen by Sartre as acts of 'pure will', of 'categorical will'—hence the extreme subjectivism and voluntarism of Sartre's 'ultra-Bolshevism'.

What compounds the dangers of Sartre's position, in Merleau-Ponty's view, is that he places this untrammelled revolutionary will in the Party. Sartre's black and white analysis allows of no gradations and, in particular, no place for working-class movements or ideas outside the Party. What is not of the Party is Other—the enemy:

> ... to pass a judgement on the CP that was a political *act* would require nothing less than the CP. Thus, by virtue of the principle of identity there is no judgement of the CP, especially not in the name of the class. At the very moment when the proletariat evades a Party-directed strike, Sartre solemnly writes that it *'recognises itself* in the test of strength which the CP institutes in its name' (AD 113).

Thus Sartre's pure subjectivism, like the pure objectivism of orthodox Marxism, ends by placing an unchallengeable possession of truth in the hands of the Party, on the basis of which also rests its right to do violence. Both positions imply a subject-object dualism, thus the negation of the 'interworld which we call history' (AD 200) and the rupturing of the dialectic of history. The dialectic is not dead. But it is not to be found, Merleau-Ponty believes, in the varieties of Marxism he has considered; nor, it is implied, in any future Marxism. Marxism has failed and must be abandoned.

However, it is not as simple as Merleau-Ponty would have us believe. Firstly, there is the question of alternatives to Marxism. In *Humanism and Terror* Marxism had been described and justified as the only possible theory and practice to give meaning to history. It might have to be rejected, but this would imply that the world was a 'senseless tumult' (HT 156), violence and irrationality inescapable and endless. When in 1955 Merleau-Ponty announced to the world that the time had now come when we could no longer wait for history to prove Marxism right, one would have expected him also to announce that we must resign ourselves to such a world. Or, alternatively, one would have expected from him some explanation as to why he no longer thought it necessary to draw such conclusions from his rejection of Marxism. But we find neither in *Adventures of the Dialectic*. All we find is a brusque and superficial rejection of his earlier position (AD 232), followed by the advocacy of a modified form of liberalism and the acceptance of a class-divided capitalist society—that is, a return to positions which he had previously argued are surpassed by Marxism.

Secondly, all kinds of issues which Merleau-Ponty had treated in *Humanism and Terror* call out for re-examination in the light of Merleau-Ponty's rejection of Marxism. But Merleau-Ponty never considers them. For example, he had previously argued that the extension of intersubjectivity and the elimination of exploitation are prerequisites for the development of meaning in history. In *Adventures of the Dialectic*, he still criticises Sartre for allowing no place for intersubjectivity in his conception of history (AD 205), so it would be interesting to know how, if intersubjectivity is still considered to be central to the dialectic, it is also now seen to be compatible with the continuation of capitalist exploitation and class struggle. Does not exploitation imply the treatment of men as objects, and hence the *negation* of intersubjectivity? If not, why not? How can the universal meaning of history develop when men are still divided—and Merleau-Ponty admits they are (AD 226–7)—into antagonistic classes?

It would also be interesting to know what Merleau-Ponty thought about the problem of violence in 1955. Revolutionary regimes, he says, are bound to be violent but this fact on its own does not imply that established capitalist regimes are any less violent than he had previously claimed. It is *possible* that they are less violent than revolutionary regimes, but Merleau-Ponty does not try to show us that this is the case and even if it were the case, the problem of violence in politics would not be eliminated. The problems of revolutionary regimes are perhaps in a large measure those of all regimes and there is nothing to suggest that Merleau-Ponty's 'new liberalism' could resolve them any better than Marxism could. As he had earlier remarked: 'Political action is of its nature impure, because it is the action of one person upon another and because it is collctive action' (HT xxxii).

In all then, Merleau-Ponty's rejection of Marxism raises as many theoretical problems within his work as he claims it resolves. As I will show in the next chapter, it also results, in practice, in his withdrawal into the liberal academic establishment and de-politicisation, since he could never find a viable alternative to Marxism.

Notes

1 See in particular 'Man and Adversity' (1951), later published in *Signs* and *In Praise of Philosophy* (1953). In both, Marxism is still assessed to be a theory in which history is the outcome of human praxis; it is still seen as a man-centred, a humanistic, theory.
2 The document written by Lenin in 1923 in which he warned against the dangers of letting power fall into Stalin's hands. It was read to the Central Committee on 22 May 1924, but was never made public (see Deutscher, 1959, Chapter 2).
3 For a good general discussion of Marx's various conceptions of the party, which shows clearly how far Marx was from Lenin's formulations, see Johnstone, 1967.
4 Lefort had already published in *Les Temps Modernes*, on his doubts about the Soviet Union, as early as 1948 (see No. 29 Feb 1948; No. 39 Dec 1948–Jan 1949). According to Sartre (1965, p. 201), Lefort was still an active associate of *Les Temps Modernes* in the early 1950s and was one of Merleau-Ponty's 'allies' against Sartre at the meetings of associates which used to take place at Sartre's flat every other Sunday.
5 De Beauvoir, in her reply to Merleau-Ponty (1955), accuses him of creating a 'pseudo-Sartre' and argues that his criticisms do not apply to the real Sartre: Sartre's is not a philosophy of the pure subject and does not ignore intersubjectivity and history, as Merleau-Ponty claims: 'Merleau-Ponty forgets only that in the authentic Sartrism there is never pure consciousness . . . Sartrean consciousness does not *exist* except insofar as it is *lost* in the world, engaged, incarnated in a body and a situation' (p. 2111. My translation).
   It seems to me that Merleau-Ponty's account of Sartrism can be considered valid as an interpretation of *Being and Nothingness*, but not of Sartre's later work. (See also on this question, Sheridan, 1968; Flynn and Howard, 1973; Descombes, 1979, pp. 64–70).

7 After Marxism

The 'Conversion' and Philosophy

IN THE last chapter, Merleau-Ponty's rejection of 'critical support' for the Soviet Union in 1950 was described as a 'conversion', precipitated by the Korean war. It was followed by a period of re-reading of the Marxist classics and a total break with Marxism by 1954, when *Adventures of the Dialectic* was written. However, to understand Merleau-Ponty's break with Marxism, it is not sufficient to remain in the realm of politics: the break has to be seen in the wider context of Merleau-Ponty's personal and general philosophical development.

On the personal front, 1952 would appear to have been a significant year. It marked the beginning of a withdrawal into private life, following Merleau-Ponty's resignation from *Les Temps Modernes* and aggravated, according to Sartre (1965, pp. 208–9) by the death of Merleau-Ponty's mother shortly after. His father had been killed in 1914, when Merleau-Ponty was about six years of age and he appears to have had a close and lasting attachment to his war-widowed mother and to have felt her death very heavily. This privatisation of Merleau-Ponty's life coincided with his appointment to probably the most illustrious—and establishment—teaching post in French philosophy, the Chair of Philosophy at the Collège de France. This was a post Bergson had once held and which, while traditionally linked to a degree of philosophical originality, was certainly not linked to radical politics. Without wishing to exaggerate the importance of these aspects of his personal life-history, they must certainly have predisposed Merleau-Ponty towards a less radical political position.

More significant, perhaps, was the evolution of Merleau-Ponty's general philosophical position from the early 1950s until his death in 1961. Since the philosophy of the *Phenom-*

enology of Perception provided the basis for Merleau-Ponty's adherence to Marxism in the 1940s, it is not surprising that the break with Marxism parallels a rejection—gradual and mainly tacit—of important aspects of that philosophy. I do not have the space to consider Merleau-Ponty's 'late' philosophy in any detail (for a work which does, see Kwant, 1966), and as it did not in fact lead to a fully worked out new political philosophy[1] it is not necessary for me to do so. However, it does constitute part of the context of his break with Marxism and it was also one of the starting points for the rather sketchy and unsatisfactory alternative political solutions he proposed in the mid-1950s. For these reasons, it merits at least some mention.

The Visible and the Invisible, on which Merleau-Ponty was working at the time of his death, was clearly intended to be a major work, of at least equal weight with the *Phenomenology of Perception*. It was a project about which he had been thinking from as early as 1952 (Pri Per 6–11), but the text left behind at his death appears to be only a fragment of the total planned. This incompleteness, together with the opacity of the content and style, make it a rather difficult book to read and discuss. Rather than making any attempt to summarise it *in toto*, I will select for mention only those aspects which I see as linked with Merleau-Ponty's change of political position.

In the *Phenomenology of Perception* and the essays of 1945–1953, it was human existence, the world as it exists for man and the world as man creates it, which provided Merleau-Ponty's main focus of concern. The source of the dialectic of existence for Merleau-Ponty was, I said, man himself, that paradoxical unity of freedom and constraint, that perpetual process of transcendence and 'unrest'. *The Visible and the Invisible* has a similar structure to that of the *Phenomenology of Perception*. The first chapters also critique various existing kinds of philosophy and call, yet again, for a new beginning, a new way of philosophising. In the last chapter (which was probably in fact the first chapter of the next section), Merleau-Ponty starts to work, as he did in *Phenomenology of Perception*, towards a new way of philosophising which should overcome the old antimonies of subject and object, being and nothingness, etc which have bedevilled European philosophy. What then is, for us, the main difference between the *Phenomenology of Perception* and *The Visible and the Invisible*?

Probably the main shift is a movement away from a man-centred or 'humanistic' conception of the world towards a conception in which Being is conceived as something infinitely vaster and more significant than human existence. For example, in the *Phenomenology of Perception*, it is man, as 'body-subject', who overcomes the dualism of subject and object. In *The Visible and the Invisible* it is claimed that this dualism, like all others, simply does not exist in fundamental or 'wild' being and is a product only of our own intellectualisations. The human body is now conceived as one 'variant' of 'carnal being' (VI 136) which is itself a 'prototype of Being', in a more universal sense—Being which is a unity, a mysterious harmony of what touches and is touched, of what sees and what is visible (VI 133–4).

Accordingly, the primary task of philosophy is no longer the interrogation of human existence. It is now seen as the disclosure of this all-embracing and mysterious Being as it *is*, and not as it appears when filtered through our conceptual frameworks and reduced to an object of thought. When we try to capture Being we distort it. The task of philosophy is the paradoxical one of saying the unsayable and thus it can only proceed indirectly, allusively, metaphorically. As Merleau-Ponty says in his discussion of dialectic: 'If one wishes to maintain its spirit it is perhaps necessary not even to name it. The sort of being to which it refers, and which we have been trying to indicate, is in fact not susceptible of being designated positively' (VI 92).

What does this new designation of the task of philosophy imply for the interpretation of history and politics? This question is not discussed in the part of *The Visible and the Invisible* which Merleau-Ponty completed, but I believe that an implicit answer underlies the new political positions he took up with his rejection of Marxism. In particular, the insistence that Being is intrinsically a harmonious unity and that human existence is but a variant of Being implies that there can be no fundamental dis-harmony in human being. The multiplicity of cultures, socio-economic systems, political systems, etc, can only be multiple expressions of a fundamental unity. Class divisions and struggle must thus become secondary phenomena, of little significance in comparison with the fundamental unity of human being.

In discussing *Humanism and Terror*, in the previous chapters, it was pointed out that there was a disjunction within Merleau-Ponty's work. On the one hand meaning, truth, creation, were considered to be the attributes of *all* human activity and the dialectic was conceived as being worked out in all human action and expression. On the other hand Merleau-Ponty argued that *only* the proletariat, as the 'universal class', could be the vehicle of the dialectic and that its liberation from exploitation was the prerequisite for a fully human society. Now this disjunction seems to be quite decisively ended with the denial of any privileged place for Marxism or the proletariat in the working out of the dialectic. As Merleau-Ponty expresses it in one of the last pieces he published, the Introduction to *Signs*, '. . . there is a flesh of history in which (as in our own body) everything counts and has a bearing . . . It [history] is of the same order as the movement of Thought and Speech, and, in short, of the perceptible world's explosion within us' (S 20).

What is significant from our point of view, in relation to political philosophy, is the assertion that 'everything counts' in history, as elsewhere in our existence. It is a point that Merleau-Ponty emphasises: '. . . it is a fact that, given our corporeal and linguistic equipment, everything we do ultimately has a meaning and a name—even if we do not know at first which one' (S 20). The implications which Merleau-Ponty takes to the world of practical politics from this position appear to be that *any* kind of politics has a worth since it is significant and that political variety, a 'pluralism' of possibilities, is desirable as best expressing both the diversity and the universality of Being and, in some unspecified way, engendering 'truth'.

The Universal in Politics

Concretely what this position implied for Merleau-Ponty was a refusal to condemn either capitalism or communism. On the contrary, he perceived a positive merit in the continued existence of the two systems: 'In world capitalism and in world communism and between the two, more truth circulates today than twenty years ago' (S 35). He argues that the dividing line between the two great systems is not clear: they form a division *within* a unity (see, for example, his article in *L'Express*, 25 6 55). In the climate of gradual East-West detente, especially with the beginning of de-Stalinisation, 'co-existence', a 'new universalism' (in *Comprendre*, September 1956, pp. 211–12) in which each system accepts the other as also possessing truth—truth being always plural—is conceived as the best solution to the world's problems, the best way to maintain the open dialectic of history.

At the level of national politics Merleau-Ponty advocates a similarly pluralistic solution, what he describes at the end of *Adventures of the Dialectic* as a 'new liberalism'. This, like Weber's 'heroic liberalism' will abandon what he regards as the superficiality and optimism of classical liberalism and accept the existence of contestation within its universe. But although Merleau-Ponty stresses that this so-called 'new liberalism' will not imply a return to the idealism of classical liberalism, that it will not be a theory which 'reduces the history of society to speculative conflicts of opinion, political struggle to exchanges of views on clearly posed problems' (AD 225), the proposals that he makes are in fact redolent of idealism.

Thus, although he says that the 'new liberalism' must recognise that there is a class struggle, must recognise the right to strike as a unique proletarian weapon and must recognise the right of the proletariat to be represented by the CP, even if it 'refuses the rules of the democratic game, since this game places it at a disadvantage' (Ad 226), these rights are to be recognised *only* if they do not threaten to overthrow the liberal order. The role of proletarian politics is to provide a limited opposition *within* the established order, against which liberalism must be able to justify its ideas:

If we speak of liberalism it is in the sense that Communist action and other revolutionary movements are accepted only as a useful menace, that we do not believe in the solution of the social problem through the power of the proletarian class or its representatives, that we expect progress only from a conscious action which will confront itself with the judgement of an opposition. Like Weber's heroic liberalism, it lets even what it contests enter its universe, and is justified in its own eyes only when it understands its opposition (AD 226).

Progress, then, is now seen occurring through the confrontation of 'judgements', through rulers having rationally to justify their actions before an opposition—in short, through the clash of ideas.

Predictably, Merleau-Ponty insists that the institution of Parliament should be the forum for this confrontation of ideas. 'Parliament', he claims, 'is the only known institution that guarantees a minimum of opposition and truth' . . . and we are back, it seems, on the territory of J. S. Mill and classical liberalism where truth emerges only through the free confrontation of ideas and all opposition is therefore tolerated—as long as it only speaks but does not act. The 'class struggle' is reduced to healthy intellectual opposition, always to be maintained within the status quo.

The reason Merleau-Ponty thinks that the class struggle should have such a circumscribed role is that capitalism is no longer what it was, so that 'political freedom is not only, and not necessarily a defence of capitalism' (AD 227). Freedom will now suffice for the development of the dialectic 'if capitalism is no longer a rigid apparatus with *its* policies, *its* ideologies, and *its* imperious laws of functioning and if, under the cover of its contradictions, another politics than *its own* can pass' (AD 227). But, one might well ask, *is* capitalism as changed as Merleau-Ponty implies? It could well be that it is, but Merleau-Ponty provides us with no grounds for saying so. Until the Epilogue, *Adventures of the Dialectic* is concerned only with Marxism and communism. The discovery that capitalism is no longer what Merleau-Ponty thought it was is a kind of *deus ex machina* suddenly introduced at the end of the book to further justify the rejection of Marxism, and Merleau-Ponty produces no justifications for this change of opinion.

Indeed, it seems to me, the main failing of Merleau-Ponty's new political position is that he arrives at it deductively, as a logical consequence of the unity of Being, and not from the study of history and society. Nowhere is it shown that capitalism is less exploitative, less violent and oppressive than it had previously been shown to be in the pages of *Les*

Temps Modernes under Merleau-Ponty's political editorship. Nowhere is the positive virtue of the perpetuation of capitalism demonstrated, except on the grounds of the *a priori*. Merleau-Ponty not only tacitly abandons phenomenology in his pursuit of Being, but ends up by falling into a crude rationalism which is totally at odds with what he claims to be his end.

Political Activity and Inactivity

In *Adventures of the Dialectic*, the 'new liberalism' is formulated as a theoretical alternative to Marxism. But for a brief period, at least, it was also a practical alternative for Merleau-Ponty. In 1954, following the French defeat in Vietnam, at Dien Bien Phu, Pierre Mendès-France came to power on a programme of negotiated de-colonisation and a revitalisation of French economic and political life. His fresh-looking domestic policies and dynamic personal political style were seen by Merleau-Ponty as a concrete expression of the 'new liberalism' and Merleau-Ponty emerged publicly—for the first and the last time after 1952—to support him. In particular, he wrote a series of articles in the newspaper *l'Express*, the semi-official organ of Mendèsism, where his appeals for 'peaceful co-existence' and a politics 'above class' in France fitted very well.

Like many other intellectuals who flocked to the support of Mendès-France, Merleau-Ponty valued his independence in advocating Keynsian policies and technocratic and interventionist approaches to the problems of the economy at a time when laissez-faire was still the orthodoxy in France. The idea—so stale today, but still novel in France in 1954—that the state, as a neutral force, should actively intervene to moderate and contain class struggle for the national good, was held out by Mendès-France as a new and non-revolutionary road to social equality and well-being. Thus:

We must reintegrate the working class into the nation and, to do this, make the nation understand that she cannot be prosperous without the prosperity of her poorest sons . . . if, in the short term, certain interests diverge, in the long term it is together that Frenchmen will be lost or saved (1955, pp. 245–6. My translation).

Linked to this position was the call for the revitalisation of French politics. Mendès-France appealed to all Frenchmen to act as citizens, beyond their own narrow class interests and to participate in the democratic process from which the decisions of the state must derive. As Merleau-Ponty put it in one of his articles in *l'Express* (23 9 54), the 'ideology of state intervention without state production . . . addresses itself to political consciousness, to the citizen as such' (my translation). Apart from its acceptance of a more active role for the state, it is hard to see how this position differs from that classical liberalism which Merleau-Ponty had so vigorously criticised in a previous period of his life.

However, with the defeat of Mendès-France in 1956 (over the question of Algeria), Merleau-Ponty's hopes for the 'new liberalism' faded. He retreated once more into private life, never again publicly to associate himself with a grouping or a platform. Increasing pessimism is the note in his last writings on politics; a pessimism strangely at odds with the affirmative tone of *The Visible and the Invisible* on which he was working. The universality and plurality of Being are unquestionable and yet—somehow—they fail to find their expression in the world of politics as they should. The alternation between faith and pessimism is most apparent in the Introduction to *Signs*. It is here that Merleau-Ponty asserts that 'everything we do has a meaning' (S 20) and talks of the growing circulation of truth between the systems of capitalism and communism. But it is also in this work that a profound pessimism about the historical and political world is displayed.

Indeed, Merleau-Ponty's starting point in the Introduction is the alarming *difference* between philosophy and history: 'If we take philosophy and history as they are being made, we shall see that philosophy finds its surest evidence at the moment of inception, and that history as it comes to be is dream or nightmare' (S 3). Later, in the discussion of the fate of Nizan,[2] Merleau-Ponty describes politics as 'a world bewitched':

Nizan had accepted force and war and death for a very clear cause; events made sport of his sacrifice, and he no longer had any sanctuary but himself. Sartre, who had believed in peace, discovered a nameless adversity which had to be clearly taken into account . . . In a world bewitched, the question is not to know who is right, who follows the truest course, but who is the match for the Great Deceiver, and what action will be tough and supple enough to bring it to reason (S 32).

What seems to happen here is a return to the themes of *Humanism and Terror*—but with Marxism no longer offering a potential way out of the individual predicament. The plight of Bukharin and Trotsky, as Merleau-Ponty portrayed it, is similar to that of Nizan; the contingency, the cruel irrationality of history, makes a mockery of the best of intentions, the clearest of understandings. But in 1947 Merleau-Ponty believed that there was a direction to history and a class with the mission of bringing about the 'recognition of man by man'. The individual's struggle was thus not seen as wholly futile. It was part of a larger movement of meaning in history, from which it derived a kind of sense, whatever happened.

It is hard to see how, had he lived, Merleau-Ponty could have extricated himself from the political inactivity into which such pessimism and resignation had tied him. Both Marxism and the 'new liberalism' having failed, he could see no other alternatives: '. . . if there is a solution to our problems it is a liberal one, and there is no longer any theoretical freedom in France', he wrote in 1958 (S 348). By the late 1950s Merleau-Ponty had aligned himself too firmly with liberal capitalism to embrace any of the 'left' alternatives to Marxism-Leninism which were developing in France, such as the growing movement for workers's self-management, Situationism, with its stress on the commodification of life under capitalism, or Henri Lefebvre's 'critique of everyday life' (see Gombin, 1975, chapters 3 and 4 for an account of the development of these alternatives in the late 1950s). One suspects that had he lived to see the events of May 1968, Merleau-Ponty would still have remained inactive, worried by the violence and the threat to stability of the revolt.

It is also hard to see how, had he continued to live, Merleau-Ponty could ever have integrated his political pessimism successfully into the framework of his new philosophy. Why is the unity and harmony of Being not manifested in the world of politics, as it surely should be?

Perhaps the answer is that the unity of Being is a philosopher's myth, an a priori construct, which, contrary to Merleau-Ponty's claims, is not rooted in the reality of human existence and thus does not find expression there. Merleau-Ponty insists, in *The Visible and the Invisible*, that the philosopher must not systematise or schematise Being and must reveal it as it *is*, in all its 'mystery'. But in his attempt at such revelation he falls into the paradoxical position of subordinating human existence to an *a priori* harmony that is not its own. Insofar as human existence does not conform to that harmony—i.e. in the world of politics—he is unable any longer to describe or account for it.

Marxism as the Disclosure of Being

Perhaps one would have expected silence from Merleau-Ponty on the subject of Marxism following the publication of *Adventures of the Dialectic*. But such is not the case. Furthermore, his treatment of Marxism is not as all-critical as one might have expected after his attack on it in *Adventures of the Dialectic*. It is yet another indication of the polemical nature of that book that in other works of this later period Merleau-Ponty treats Marxism with much more respect. However, this respect is accompanied by the total depoliticisation of Marxism. It is reduced to one of the 'classics' of philosophy and to a forerunner of Merleau-Ponty's own new philosophy. In the same way that Marxism had earlier been proclaimed to be a variant of the 'philosophy of existence', it is now proclaimed to be primarily an ontology, a 'disclosure' of Being similar to that which Merleau-Ponty was developing. As both 'classic' and ontology Marxism becomes wholly disconnected from any notion of class struggle or revolutionary practice.

A 'classic', says Merleau-Ponty, is a philosophy which remains a 'secondary' truth, even though it has been superseded by more recent and truer formulations. Such, wrote Merleau-Ponty in 1960, is Marxism. It is too simplistic to say either that Marxism is 'true' or that it is 'false'. It is too simplistic to say that it is 'still valid' or that it is 'contradicted by the facts' (S 9–10). Marxism, like all thought, is both true *and* false. The 'error' Marx makes 'is not simply the converse of truth but rather a truth that failed . . . Marx's theses can remain true as the Pythagorean theorem is true: no longer in the sense it was true for the one who invented it—as an immutable truth and a property of space itself—but as a property of a certain model of space among other possible spaces' (S 10). It is the distinguishing quality of a 'secondary truth' or 'classic' that it cannot ever be ignored or wholly rejected, even though we can go beyond it.

Are you or are you not a Cartesian? The question does not make much sense, since those who reject this or that in Descartes do so only in terms of reasons that owe a lot to Descartes. We say that Marx is in the process of becoming such a secondary truth (S 11).

Are you or are you not a Marxist? Do you criticise Marxism 'from within or without'? Such questions, Merleau-Ponty asserts, no longer have a meaning and cannot be answered. For Marxism is no longer a new doctrine or an historical movement, but '. . . an immense field of sedimented history and thought where one goes to practice and to learn to think' (S 12). We can still use Marxist categories to describe the world; the problems which Marxism points to and the 'frame of reference' from which it 'discloses' the world's problems cannot be ignored. But such a theoretical Marxism is only one of the possible frames of reference and no longer provides us with policies or guidelines for action, as it did Marx:

The relationship between philosophy and history is less simple than was believed. It is in a strict sense *action at a distance*, each from the depth of its difference requiring intermingling and promiscuity. We have yet to learn the proper uses of this encroachment (S 13).

Marxism thus ends, for Merleau-Ponty, by becoming part of the process of the disclosure of Being, one 'classic' philosophy among others—and yet clearly it is more significant for Merleau-Ponty than some others remain. For although in its own terms, as revolutionary praxis, Marxism has, Merleau-Ponty believes, been rendered less and less relevant by time, as philosophy, as the 'disclosure of Being', it has the unique strength of conceiving of a unity of Being which precedes the distinctions of subjective and objective, matter and consciousness. As Merleau-Ponty becomes increasingly concerned with ontology and with the 'mystery' of Being, the significance of Marxism is also reduced in his eyes to its ontological implications. Marxism as 'praxis', as men making history through the process of class struggle, is dismissed as erroneous rationalism, while the philosophical underpinnings of this 'praxis' are preserved as a prototype of Merleau-Ponty's own philosophy of Being.

It is above all in the preparatory notes to Merleau-Ponty's last lecture course (in *Textures*, No. 10–11, 1975) that we find the embryo of this interpretation of Marxism as a philosophy of Being. The notes are dense and the argument interrupted by Merleau-Ponty's death. Even so, the main points of the new reading of Marx emerge. Marx's philosophy is 'essentially dialectical', which is to say, like the philosophy of *The Visible and the Invisible*, it starts from a concept of Being which *precedes* all dualisms:

> . . . nature and men and history are all understood not as substances definable by a principal attribute, but as movements without a locatable discontinuity, where the other is always implied. No separation of matter-idea, object-subject, nature-man, in itself-for itself, but one single Being where negativity works (p. 168).

Within this dialectical movement nature cannot be defined as a pure object, but becomes for Marx 'the "sensible", the fleshly, nature as we see it', and man is neither a pure subject nor an objective fragment of nature, but 'a sort of Subject-Object coupling', an 'active object'. He is thereby also necessarily in relationship to other men, a species-being: 'this relation being the transformation and continuation of the natural relation of the living to external beings. History being in this sense the very flesh of man' (p. 168).

Marx, Merleau-Ponty says, failed to maintain this dialectical philosophy and ended by asserting the possibility of a 'true' essence of man under communism, hence after all, the 'end of history' and the reign of 'positivity'. But even so, the non-dualistic concept of Being from which Marx started was a great advance on any previous philosophy and, indeed, an earlier and more fumbling evocation of what Merleau-Ponty himself is trying to develop. Since Merleau-Ponty denies that it makes sense to ask who is or is not a Marxist or which view is 'inside' Marxism and which 'outside' it, he can reduce Marxism to the 'disclosure of Being' without feeling that he is distorting its main significance: Marx was mistaken insofar as he believed that the main significance of his writings was their revolutionary implication. Without his ever having been aware of the fact, Marx's main significance is as an ontologist.

However, Merleau-Ponty's views are not quite as consistent as they might appear. For what is implied in this selective approach to Marxism which ignores what Marx himself thought, is an abandonment of a phenomenological approach to the history of ideas—an approach which is still implicit in the conception of philosophy as the 'disclosure of being'. Hegel, Merleau-Ponty had once said, remained a student of concrete existence, hence phenomenological in his approach, only insofar as he studied epochs for their *intrinsic* value and not solely as stages in the process of the unfolding of the Absolute (SNS 64). As soon as he studies Marx only for what he can contribute to a particular ontology and no longer for his own intrinsic significance, Merleau-Ponty, even while talking of philosophy as 'disclosure of Being', contradicts himself and engages in God-like survey, a 'high altitude' reconstruction, of the history of philosophy.

Merleau-Ponty is well aware that such is *not* the kind of history of philosphy which is implied in his new philosophy. In a working note for *The Visible and the Invisible* in 1959, he wrote the following:

In accordance with the idea of transcendence . . . seek to define a history of philosophy that would not be a flattening of history into 'my' philosophy —and that would not be idolatry . . . The history of philosophy as a *perception* of other philosophers, intentional encroachment upon them, a thought of one's own that does not kill them either by overcoming them. or by copying them (VI 198).

Yet, in his treatment of Marx in the following year, Merleau-Ponty fails—yet again—to follow his own recommendations. For what he does *is* to 'flatten' Marx into his own philosophy. One could not think of a better word to describe the process in which the significance of Marxism is reduced only to that which is relevant to Merleau-Ponty's own philosophy.

Notes

1 Merleau-Ponty intimated in 1960 that he did intend to work through the political implications of his new philosophy: 'Like all philosophy, that which we must seek will inspire a politics' he told an interviewer (Chapsal, 1960, p. 161). Asked whether he would write any more books on politics, he replied: 'The political philosophy will come with the rest' (ibid., p. 163). (My translation.)
2 Paul Nizan, graduate of the Ecole Normale, author of *Aden, Arabie, Le Conspiration, Les Chiens de Garde* and *Antoine Bloyé*; known as an 'angry young man' of the 1930s.

   A few years older than Merleau-Ponty, Nizan was a communist militant for many years. He left the PCF in 1939 over the Hitler-Stalin pact, for which he continued to be vilified by the PCF even after his death in 1940, at the hands of the Nazis.

   Sartre wrote a preface to *Aden, Arabie* when it was republished by Maspero in 1960. It is that preface which provides the text for Merleau-Ponty's discussion of Sartre and Nizan.

Concluding Remarks

THERE is much more that could be said. Merleau-Ponty's philosophy is profound enough to warrant a virtually unending process of exploration. There are themes I have only touched on, or even ignored. But even those themes which have been dealt with at some length have not been—could not have been—dealt with, in any sense, fully. I have tried, however, to reveal both the continuities and the disjunctures; to reveal the overall coherence of Merleau-Ponty's approach to the world and to politics, but also those places where he became inconsistent. By focusing explicitly on the political themes and bringing together, as one body, ideas which previously were scattered throughout Merleau-Ponty's life's writings, I have, I hope, clarified them somewhat and shown them to have, in general, a coherence which perhaps was not visible when they were isolated from each other.

The source of that coherence, I have shown, is to be found in Merleau-Ponty's rejection of rationalism (of either the idealist or the positivist variety), and his insistence that human existence can only be understood if it is grasped as it is 'perceived' by our bodies prior to the operations of consciousness—that is 'concretely', or phenomenologically. It was from this fundamental insight that Merleau-Ponty came to criticise liberalism as a rationalism and to identify his own ideas with those of Marxism, as a 'lived' philosophy. It was from much the same position—ableit reformulated in more metaphysical tones—that he later came to reject Marxism as also being a rationalism.

But although this fundamental insight unified his general philosophy and his political philosophy and linked together the elements of the latter, certain inner tensions still remained within Merleau-Ponty's political ideas. One of these, the tension between the universalistic conception of the genesis of meaning implied in his fundamental insight and the emphasis in the Marxism he embraced on the proletariat as the vehicle of meaning, was resolved, by 1954, with his move away from Marxism. Never resolved, however, was the contradiction between, on the one hand, Merleau-Ponty's criticism of rationalism and of the detached philosophy of a 'surveying consciousness' and, on the other hand, his own repeated use of such rationalistic and 'surveying' methods. Found in his arbitrary and abstract critique of liberalism in the 1940s and still apparent in his treatment of Marxism in his last lecture notes, Merleau-Ponty's tendency to treat the ideas of others over-abstractly, as mere steps in a process of development or an argument, runs directly counter to his advocacy of a method which treats all ideas as *intrinsically* significant and his argument that the task of the phenomenological philosopher is to attempt to understand ideas—and indeed all human action and 'institution'—in terms of their significance for their authors.

But in spite of these internal contradictions, Merleau-Ponty's political philosophy has much to offer us. Not answers, though. He leaves unanswered most of the important questions he raises. The possibility of moral action in politics, the direction of history, the possibility of eliminating violence—all are still open questions at the end of his analysis. This is not, however, a weakness of his work. Perhaps the main lesson to be drawn from Merleau-Ponty's political philosophy is that the debate can never be definitively closed. A politics of universal principles, such as classical liberalism, or its Marxist equivalent, what one might call the politics of the 'right line' (which assumes that if Marxist science is correctly applied, there exists *the* correct analysis to be discovered, from which *the* correct political line can be deduced), both fall into an over-simplistic rationalism. Not only are there no universal principles, but there are no wholly 'correct' answers to political questions. It is not simply a matter of applying Marxism correctly to come up with the correct answers and the 'right line'. Political analyses are never simply true or false, political decisions never wholly right or wrong.

If Merleau-Ponty does not offer us answers to the questions about politics he raises, what does he offer us? Above all he offers us, to use his own word, a particular way of *perceiving* politics. A way which refuses to over-simplify and which locates politics within the broader dialectic of human existence. He urges on us the need not to divorce politics from other aspects of our existence, to consider and engage in it as an aspect of the 'totality' of life, a totality whose basis is the intrinsically intersubjective nature of our being. This perception of politics, which Merleau-Ponty developed in the 1940s, although it has rarely been articulated since, has been a fundamental starting point for important political currents in the 1960s and 1970s, which have argued for the need to look at the 'political' aspects of areas of life traditionally labelled as 'non-political', such as the family (Laing, 1969) or our everyday use of language (Pateman, 1975).

It is perhaps ironic that while movements have flourished on the European Left which have rejected the orthodox Marxist emphasis on the political and economic struggle, basing themselves instead on the fundamental premises of the unity of human existence in general and the unity of the life experience of the individual (one can mention such examples as Situationism in France, the Provos in Holland, movements for 'alternative' theatre, psychiatry, education in Britain and the women's movement across Western Europe), French philosophy, including Marxist philosophy, turned its back on these premises in the 1960s. 'Structuralism', with its stress on the autonomy of structures, linguistic or social, from the meanings men invest in them is (as a gross generalisation) the attempt to *decompose* human existence. It focuses on life not as a totality, but as an aggregate of disparate forms.

In the work of Althusser, structuralist premises are used to divide up political reality into separated, non-communicating segments: lived experience is able to give us only 'ideology', while Marxism, as a 'science', can have its basis only in 'theoretical practice' (1969, 1970), which is divorced from other kinds of practice. Althusser's analysis of Marxism is in many ways the antithesis of Merleau-Ponty's. In spite of the acclaim accorded to Althusser by certain Marxist intellectuals in both France and Britain, much recent political activity has in fact continued to have as its unspoken basis the view of politics and human existence which Merleau-Ponty formulated so clearly more than three decades ago.

Chronology

Year	Events in Merleau-Ponty's life	Merleau-Ponty's main publications	Significant political events	Significant intellectual events
1908	Born, Rochefort-sur-Mer.			
1914	Father killed in action.		Outbreak of World War One.	
1917			Russian Revolution.	
1927	Entered Ecole Normale to read philosophy.			Heidegger: *Being and Time*. Marcel: *Metaphysical Journal*.
1928	Probably heard Gurvitsch lecture.			Gurvitsch: lectures at the Ecole Normale on Husserl and Heidegger (also in 1929 and 1930).
1929	Probably heard Husserl lecture.			Husserl: 'Paris lectures'.
1930	Graduated from Ecole Normale (October). Military service.			
1931	Took up post of philosophy teacher, Lycée Mixte, Beauvais (October).			Husserl: *Cartesian Meditations*.
1933			Hitler to power in Germany.	Kojève lecturing on Hegel at Ecole des Hautes Etudes (continued until 1939).

Year			
1934	Registered titles of two doctoral theses on perception. Took up teaching post at lycée in Chartres.		Sartre studying phenomenology in Berlin.
1935	Took up junior teaching post at Ecole Normale (held until 1939).	First publication: 'Christianisme et ressentiment', in *La Vie Intellectuelle*.	Marcel: *Being and Having*.
1936		Review of Marcel's *Être et Avoir* in *La Vie Intellectuelle*.	Outbreak of Spanish Civil War
			Sartre: *The Transcendence of the Ego* and *The Imagination*. Husserl: *Crisis* (incomplete). Husserl Archives established at Louvain.
1938	Completed manuscript of *The Structure of Behaviour*.		
1939	Visited Husserl Archives (April). Called up (September).		Outbreak of World War Two (September).
1940	Demobilised (September). Took up teaching post in Paris at Lycée Carnot (until 1944).		German occupation of Paris (June).
1941	In 'Socialisme et Liberté', Resistance group, with Sarte (April–October).		

Year	Events in Merleau-Ponty's life	Merleau-Ponty's main publications	Significant political events	Significant intellectual events
1942		The Structure of Behaviour.		
1943				Sartre: Being and Nothingness.
1944			Liberation of Paris. De Gaulle established provisional government (Aug.).	
1945	Took up post as Professor of Philosophy, University of Lyon.	Phenomenology of Perception.	'Tripartism'—Catholic, Socialist and Communist coalition government in France. Outbreak of war of independence in Indo-China. Riots in Algeria (at Sétif).	Les Temps Modernes founded (first issue in October). Merleau-Ponty was political editor.
1946			Bombing of Haiphong (Nov.).	Les Temps Modernes began explicitly anti-colonialist stand (December editorial).
1947		Humanism and Terror.	Winter of shortages and inflation. Strikes. Communists dismissed from government for supporting strikes—end of 'Tripartism' (May). Launching of Marshall Aid.	

1948	Merleau-Ponty joined R.D.R. but, unlike Sartre, was not active.	*Sense and Non-Sense.*	Coup in Czechoslovakia (Feb.). Start of Berlin blockade (June). Le Rassemblement Démocratique et Révolutionnaire (R.D.R.) founded (March).
1949	Took up post of Professor of Philosophy at the Sorbonne.		North Atlantic Treaty signed (April). People's Republic of China established (October). Collapse of R.D.R. (summer-autumn).
1950	With war in Korea, demanded silence on political issues from *Les Temps Modernes*.		Outbreak of Korean War (July).
1952	Took up Chair of Philosophy at the Collège de France. Death of mother. Resigned from *Les Temps Modernes*.		Sartre: *The Communists and Peace.*
1953		*In Praise of Philosophy* (inaugural lecture).	Armistice in Korea (July).

Year	Events in Merleau-Ponty's life	Merleau-Ponty's main publications	Significant political events	Significant intellectual events
1954	Gave public support to Mendès-France	Articles in *L'Express*.	Start of Mendès-France administration (June), following French defeat Dien Bien Phu. Full-scale insurrection in Algeria.	
1955		*Adventures of the Dialectic*. Articles in *L'Express*.	Fall of Mendès-France administration (Feb.).	
1956	Participated in East-West cultural conference in Venice (March).	*Les Philosophes Célèbres* (ed.).	Russia: Twentieth Congress (Feb.). Hungarian uprising (October). Suez invasion (Oct.).	
1958			Collapse of Fourth Republic. De Gaulle became Premier (May).	
1960		*Signs*.	First French A-Bomb exploded.	
1961	Died 4 May.			Sartre: *Critique of Dialectical Reason*.

Bibliography One

Works by Merleau-Ponty referred to in the text

WORKS are listed chronologically, according to the date of publication of the French originals. Where appropriate, details of the English translation used are given in brackets.

1942
La Structure du Comportement, Presses Universitaires de France, Paris. The manuscript for this book was completed in 1938. (*The Structure of Behaviour*, trans. A. Fisher, Methuen, London, 1965).

1945
Phénoménologie de la Perception, Gallimard, Paris. (*Phenomenology of Perception*, trans. C. Smith, Routledge and Kegan Paul, London, 1962).

1947
Humanisme et Terreur, Gallimard, Paris. This work consisted of a revised and expanded version of a series of essays which had appeared in *Les Temps Modernes*, under the title 'Le Yogi et le Prolétaire', in the issues of October 1946, November 1946, January 1947 and July 1947. (*Humanism and Terror*, trans. J. O'Neill, Beacon Press, Boston, USA, 1969).

'Le primat de la perception et ses conséquences philosophiques', *Bulletin de la Société Française de Philosophie*, XLI, Dec 1947. ('The primacy of perception and its philosophical consequences', trans. J. M. Edie, in the collection *The Primacy of Perception and Other Essays*, ed J. M. Edie, Northwestern UP, Evanston, USA, 1964).

1948
Sens et Non-Sens, Nagel, Paris. A collection of essays previously published in various journals between 1945 and 1947. A large number of the essays had appeared in *Les Temps Modernes*. (*Sense and Non-Sense*, trans. H. L. Dreyfus and P. A. Dreyfus, Northwestern UP, Evanston, USA, 1964).

1953
Eloge de la Philosophie, Gallimard, Paris. Merleau-Ponty's inaugural lecture, on taking up the Chair of Philosophy at the 'Collège de France'. (*In Praise of Philosophy*, trans. J. Wild and J. M. Edie, Northwestern UP, Evanston, USA, 1963).

'Les relations avec autrui chez l'enfant, première partie', *Les Cours du Sorbonne*, Tournier et Constants, Paris. ('The Child's Relations with Others', trans. W. Cobb, in *The Primacy of Perception and Other Essays*, ed J. M. Edie, Northwestern UP, Evanston, USA, 1964).

1954
'La France va-t-elle se renouveler?', *L'Express*, 23 Oct.

1955
Les Adventures de la Dialectique, Gallimard, Paris. (*Adventures of the Dialectic*, trans. J. Bien, Heinemann, London, 1974).

'Ou va l'anticommunisme?', *L'Express*, 25 June.

1956
Les Philosophes Célèbres (editor), Mazenod, Paris.

'Recontres est-ouest à Venise', transcript of a conference in which Merleau-Ponty participated in March 1956, published in *Comprendre*, Vol XVI, Venice, Sept.

1960
Signes, Gallimard, Paris. A collection of essays previously published in a variety of journals between 1949 and 1959. (*Signs*, trans. R. C. McClearly, Northwestern UP, Evanston, USA, 1964).

1964
Le Visible et l'Invisible, edited by C. Lefort, Gallimard, Paris. Incomplete text on which Merleau-Ponty was working at the time of his death in 1961. (*The Visible and the Invisible*, trans. A. Lingis, Northwestern UP, Evanston, USA, 1968).

1968
Resumés de Cours, Collège de France, 1952–1960, Gallimard, Paris. (*Themes from the Lectures*, trans. J. O'Neill, Northwestern UP, Evanston, USA, 1970).

1975
'Philosophie et Non-Philosophie depuis Hegel (II). Notes de cours', edited by C. Lefort, *Textures*, No. 10–11, Belgium.

Bibliography Two

Other works referred to in the text

Where English translations of French works are listed, details of their publication in French are given in brackets.

Alain (1956) *Propos*, Vol 1, ed. M. Savin, Gallimard, Paris.
Althusser, L. (1969) *For Marx*, trans. B. Brewster, New Left Books, London. (*Pour Marx*, Maspero, Paris, 1965).
Althusser, L. and Balibar, E. (1970) *Reading Capital*, trans. B. Brewster, New Left Books, London. (*Lire Le Capital*, Maspero, Paris, 1965).
Anon. (1946) Review of *Phenomenology of Perception*, *Times Literary Supplement*, 2 March, 1946.
Arendt, H. (1970) *On Violence*, Allen Lane, London.
Bachelard, G. (1947) *La Poétique de l'Espace*, Presses Universitaires Françaises, Paris.
Barral, M. (1965) *Merleau-Ponty: the Role of the Body-Subject in Interpersonal Relations*, Duquesne University Press, Pittsburgh, U.S.A.
De Beauvoir, S. (1955) 'Merleau-Ponty et le pseudo-sartrisme,' *Les Temps Modernes*, Nos. 114–5, May, 1955.
De Beauvoir, S. (1963) *The Prime of Life*, trans. P. Green, André Deutsch and Weidenfeld and Nicolson, London. (*La Force de l'Age*, Gallimard, Paris, 1960).
De Beauvoir, S. (1965) *Force of Circumstance*, trans. R. Howe, André Deutsch and Weidenfeld and Nicolson, London. (*La Force des Choses*, Gallimard, Paris, 1963).
Brunschvicg, L. (1931) *De La Connaissance de Soi*, Librairie Félix Alcan, Paris.
Van Breda, H. L. (1962) 'Merleau-Ponty et les Archives-Husserl à Louvain,' *Revue de Métaphysique et de Morale*, Vol 67, October–December, 1962.
Burnier, M.-A. (1966) *Les Existentialistes et la Politique*, Gallimard, Paris.

Chapsal, M. (1960) *Les Ecrivains en Personne*, Julliard, Paris.
Cliff, T. (1964) *Russia: a Marxist Analysis*, International Socialism, London.
Descombes, V. (1979) *Le Même et l'Autre: Quarante-cinq ans de philosophie française (1933–1978)*, Editions de Minuit, Paris and Cambridge University Press.
Deutscher, I. (1959) *The Prophet Unarmed. Trotsky: 1921–1929*, Oxford University Press.
Djilas, M. (1966) *The New Class*, Unwin, London.
Dzelepy, E. N. (1949) 'Les "democraties en action", ou du pétrole sur l'Acropole,' *Les Temps Modernes*, No. 48, October, 1949.
Flynn, B. (1973) 'The Question of Ontology,' *Horizons of the Flesh*, ed. G. Gillan, Southern Illinois University Press, Carbondale, U.S.A.
Garaudy, R. (1970) *The Turning Point of Socialism*, trans. P. and B. Ross, Fontana, London. (*Le Grand Tournant du Socialisme*, Gallimard, Paris, 1970).
Goldstein, K. (1934) *Der Aufbau des Organismus*, Martinus Nijhoff, The Hague.
Gombin, R. (1975) *The Origins of Modern Leftism*, Penguin, Harmondsworth. (*Les Origines du Gauchisme*, Editions du Seuil, Paris, 1971).
Gramsci, A. (1971) *Prison Notebooks*, trans. Q. Hoare and G. Nowell Smith, International Publishers, New York.
Hegel, G. F. (1967) *The Philosophy of Right*, trans. T. M. Knox, Oxford University Press.
Hegel, G. F. (1971) *Phenomenology of Mind*, trans. J. B. Baillie, George Allen and Unwin, London.
Howard, D. (1973) 'Ambiguous Radicalism,' *Horizons of the Flesh*, ed. G. Gillan, Southern Illinois University Press, Carbondale, U.S.A.
Husserl, E. (1961) *Cartesian Meditations*, trans. D. Cairns, Martinus Nijhoff, The Hague. (The French translation, by G. Peiffer and E. Levinas, appeared in 1931, Armand Colin, Paris).
Husserl, E. (1970) *The Crisis of the European Sciences and Transcendental Phenomenology*, trans. D. Carr, Northwestern University Press, Evanston, U.S.A. (German edition, ed. W. Biemel, Martinus Nijhoff, The Hague, 1954).
Hyppolite, J. (1935) 'Les travaux de jeunesse de Hegel d'après des ouvrage récents,' *Revue de Métaphysique et de Morale*, Vol. 42, July and October, 1935.
Hyppolite, J. (1971) 'L'Existence dans la "Phénoménologie" de Hegel,' *Figures de la Pensée Philosophiques*, Vol 1, Presses Universitaires Françaises, Paris.

Johnstone, M. (1967) 'Marx and Engels and their Concept of the Party,' *Socialist Register,* Merlin Press, London.
Kamenka, E. (1962) *The Ethical Foundations of Marxism,* Routledge and Kegan Paul, London.
Koehler, W. (1930) *Gestalt Psychology,* G. Bell, London.
Koffka, K. (1925) *The Growth of Mind,* Kegan Paul, London.
Kojève, A. (1962) *Introduction to the Reading of Hegel,* trans. J. H. Nichols Jr., Basic Books, Inc., New York. (*Introduction à la Lecture de Hegel,* ed.R. Queneau, Gallimard, Paris, 1947).
Korsch, K. (1972) *Marxism and Philosophy,* trans. F. Halliday, New Left Books, London.
Koyré, A. (1931) 'Rapport sur l'Etat des Etudes Hégéliennes en France,' *Revue d'Histoire de la Philosophie,* Vol. 5, 1931.
Koyré, A. (1934) 'Hegel à Iena,' *Revue d'Histoire et de Philosophie Religieuses,* 1934. Reprinted in *Etudes d'Histoire de la Pensée Philosophique,* Armand Colin, Paris, 1961.
Kwant, R. (1963) *The Phenomenological Philosophy of Merleau-Ponty,* Duquesne University Press, Pittsburgh, U.S.A.
Kwant, R. (1966) *From Phenomenology to Metaphysics,* Duquesne University Press, Pittsburgh, U.S.A.
Laing, R. D. (1962) *The Politics of the Family,* CBC Publications, New York.
Lavelle, L. (1939) 'Avant Propos,' in Le Senne, R., *Introduction à la Philosophie,* Presses Universitaires Françaises, Paris.
Lefort, C. (1948) 'Kravchenko et le problème de l'URSS,' *Les Temps Modernes,* No. 29, February, 1948.
Lefort, C. (1948–1949). 'La contradiction de Trotsky et le problème révolutionnaire,' *Les Temps Modernes,* No. 39, December, 1948–January, 1949.
Lefort, C. (1952) 'Le prolétariat et sa direction,' *Socialisme ou Barbarie,* No. 10, July–August, 1952. (Reprinted in Lefort, C., *Eléments d'une Critique de la Bureaucratie,* Droz, Geneva, 1971, pp. 30–8).
Lefort,C. (1963) 'La Politique et la Pensée de la Politique,' *Lettres Nouvelles,* 11th year, new series, No. 32, February, 1963.
Lefort, C. (1974) 'Preface' to *The Prose of the World,* Heinemann, London.
Lenin, V. I. (1960) 'What is to be Done?', *Selected Works,* Vol. 1, Moscow.
Lukacs, G. (1948) *Existentialisme ou Marxisme?,* Nagel, Paris.
Lukacs, G. (1971) *History and Class Consciousness,* trans. R. Livingstone, Merlin Press, London. (*Geschichte und Klassenbewusstsein,* 1923).
Marcel, G. (1935) *Etre et Avoir,* Aubier, Paris.

Marx, K. (1959) *Economic and Philosophical Manuscripts*, trans. M. Milligan, Lawrence and Wishart, London.
Marx, K. (1964) *Early Writings*, ed. T. Bottomore, McGraw Hill, New York.
Marx, K. (1965) *The German Ideology*, trans. and ed. C. J. Arthur, Lawrence and Wishart, London.
Marx, K. (1970a) *Capital*, Vol 1, trans. S. Moore and E. Aveling, Lawrence and Wishart, London.
Marx, K. (1970b) *Critique of Hegel's Philosophy of Right*, trans. A. Jolin and J. O'Malley, Cambridge University Press.
Marx, K. (1971) *Grundrisse*, ed. D. McLellan, Macmillan, London.
Marx, K. (1973) *Surveys from Exile*, ed. D. Fernbach, Allen Lane, London.
Mays, W. (1975) 'Phenomenology and Marxism,' *Phenomenology and Philosophical Understanding*, ed. E. Pivcevic, Cambridge University Press.
Mendès-France, P. (1955) *P. Mendès-France: Sept Mois et Dix-Sept Jours*, Julliard, Paris.
Mészáros, I. (1970) *Marx's Theory of Alienation*, Merlin Press, London.
Minkowski, E. (1933). *Le Temps Vécu. Etudes Phénoménologiques et Psychopathologiques*, Collection de l'Evolution Psychiatrique, Paris.
Paci, E. (1972) *The Function of the Sciences and the Meaning of Man*, trans. P. Piccone and J. E. Hansen, Northwestern University Press, Evanston, U.S.A. (Italian original 1963.)
Pateman, T. (1975) *Language, Truth and Politics*, Stroud and Pateman, private publication, Sidmouth, England.
Pavlov, I. V. (1964) *Lectures on Conditioned Reflexes*, (2 Vols), trans. and ed. W. Horsley Gantt, Lawrence and Wishart, London. (Original English translation 1928; first Russian edition 1923).
Piccone, P. (1971) 'Phenomenological Marxism,' *Telos*, Vol 4, No. 9, 1971.
Ricoeur, P. (1967) *Husserl. An analysis of his phenomenology*, Northwestern University Press, Evanston, U.S.A.
Rovatti, P. (1970) 'A Phenomenological Analysis of Marxism,' *Telos*, Vol. 2, No. 5, 1970.
Sartre, J.-P. (1948) 'Les Mains Sales,' *Les Temps Modernes*, Nos. 30-1, March–April, 1948.
Sartre, J.-P. (1965) 'Merleau-Ponty,' *Situations*, trans. B. Eisler, Fawcett Publications, Connecticut, U.S.A. ('Merleau-Ponty Vivant,' *Les Temps Modernes*, No. 184, October, 1961).
Sartre, J.-P. (1966) *Being and Nothingness*, trans. H. E. Barnes,

Washington Square Press, New York. (*L'Etre et le Néant*, Gallimard, Paris, 1943).

Sartre, J.-P. (1969) *The Communists and Peace*, trans. I. Clephane, Hamish Hamilton, London. ('Les Communistes et la Paix,' *Les Temps Modernes*, Nos. 81 and 84–5 (July and October–November, 1952) and No. 89 (April, 1953).

Sartre, J.-P. (1976) *Critique of Dialectical Reason*, trans. A. Sheridan-Smith, New Left Books, London. (*Critique de la Raison Dialectique*, Gallimard, Paris, 1960).

Sheridan, J. F. (1968) 'Ontology and Politics: A Polemic,' *Dialogue* (Canada), Vol. 7, 1968.

Smart, B. (1976) *Sociology, Phenomenology and Marxian Analysis*, Routledge and Kegan Paul, London.

Spiegelberg, H. (1960) *The Phenomenological Movement. A Historical Introduction* (2 Vols), Martinus Nijhoff, The Hague.

Tran-Duc-Thao (1971) *Phénoménologie et Materialisme Dialectique*, Gordon Breach, Paris.

Trotsky, L. (1945) *The Revolution Betrayed*, Pioneer Publishers, New York.

De Waelhens, A. (1951) *Une Philosophie de l'Ambiguité*, Publications Universitaires de Louvain, Louvain, Belgium.

Wahl, J. (1929) *Le Malheur de la Conscience dans la Philosophie de Hegel*, Editions Rieder, Paris.

Wahl, J. (1932) *Vers le Concret*, Vrin, Paris.

Index

Adventures of the Dialectic, 61, 103, 108, 112, 113, 115, 117, 118, 123, 124, 125, 128
Alain, 62, 63, 64, 67–8, 73, 74, 76, 87
Althusser, L., 135
Arendt, H., 80

Bachelard, G., 66
Barral, M., 23n

De Beauvoir, S., xivn, 3, 61, 76, 118n
Being and Nothingness, (Sartre), 14, 34–5, 76, 118n
Bergson, H., 119
Van Breda, H. L., 8
Brunschvicg, L., 3, 73
Bukharin, N., 39–40, 41n, 88–90, 127
Burnier, M.-A., xivn

Capital, (Marx), 48–9, 57
Cartesian Meditations, (Husserl), 8
Cézanne, 37
Chapsal, M., 3, 132
Cliff, T., 109
Cold War, 63, 69
Collège de France, 28, 119
Communists and Peace, The, (Sartre), 115
Comprendre, 123
Crisis, The, (Husserl), 8–9, 26
Critique of Dialectical Reason, (Sartre), 35

Descartes, R., 6, 7, 23n, 26
Descombes, V., 25, 118n
Deutscher, I., 118n
Dialectics of Nature, (Engels), 47–8
Djilas, M. 109
Dzelepy, E. N., xii

Economic and Philosophic Manuscripts, (Marx), 45
Engels, F., 47, 105
Existentialisme ou Marxisme?, (Lukacs), 56–7
Express, L', 123, 125–6

Flynn, B., 118n
France, 4, 69, 70, 73, 96, 101, 125, 127
Frankfurt School, 45
French Communist Party (PCF), xii, 38, 45–6, 60, 91, 96, 116, 123

Garaudy, R., 45
German Ideology, The, (Marx), 50
German occupation (of France), xi, 20, 46, 58, 62, 63, 64–5, 88, 96
Gilson, E., 3
Goldstein, K., 6
Gombin, R., 127
Gramsci, A., 45

Hegel, G. F., 4, 9, 16, 20, 24–41, 46, 47, 50, 52, 53, 78–9, 83, 87–8, 113, 131
Heidegger, M., 4
Helvétius, C., 73
Hervé, P., 57
History and Class Consciousness, (Lukacs), 57
Howard, D., 118n
Humanism and Terror, xii, 38–40, 46–7, 70, 83, 85, 90, 92, 107–8, 109–10, 116–17, 122, 127
Husserl, E., 4, 7–9, 11, 14, 25–6
Hyppolite, J., 25–7

Indo-China, *see* Vietnam

Johnstone, M., 118n

Index

Kamenka, E., 97n
Kant, I., 6, 26, 29
Koehler, W., 6
Koffka, K., 6
Kojève, A., 4, 25–6, 31
Korean War, 101–2
Korsch, K., 45, 105
Koyré, A., 4, 25
Kwant, R., 23n, 120

Laing, R. D., 135
Laval, P., 88–9, 97n
Lavelle, L., 3, 23n
Lefebvre, H., 127
Lefort, C., 58–9, 85, 103, 112, 118n
Lenin, V. I., 47, 54, 92, 93–4, 104–6, 108, 110–12, 118n
Locke, J., 74
Logic (Hegel), 28
Lukacs, G., 45, 56–7, 103, 104–7

Machiavelli, N., 63
Mains Sales, Les, (Sartre), 86
Marcel, G., 4
Marshall aid, xii
Marx, K., 21, 36, 38, 45–60, 63, 74, 78, 83–4, 86, 92, 103, 106, 109–10, 112, 113, 114, 115, 115–16, 118n, 129, 130–2
Materialism and Empirio-Criticism, (Lenin), 47–8, 104
May Events of 1968, xiii–xiv, 127
Mays, W., 60
Mendès-France, P., 125–6
Mészáros, I., 97n
Mill, J. S., 124
Minkowski, E., 4
Montesquieu, C., 73

Nazi occupation, *see* German occupation (of France)
Nizan, P., 126–7, 132n

Paci, E., 60
Pateman, T., 135
Pavlov, I. V., 5
Pétain, P., 88–9, 97n
Phenomenology of Mind, The, (Hegel), 25–8, 33

Phenomenology of Perception, xi, 5, 7, 12, 13, 14–15, 18–19, 20–2, 24, 32, 37, 51, 59, 77, 78–9, 85, 106, 119–21
Philosophy of History, (Hegel), 31
Philosophy of Right, The, (Hegel), 28, 31
Piccone, P., 60

Radical Party, 67
Resistance, xi, 46
Ricoeur, P., 7
Rovatti, P., 60
Russian Revolution, 40, 86, 90, 92, 114

Sartre, J.-P., xi–xiii, 3, 14, 18, 23n, 33, 34–5, 56, 58, 76, 86, 101–3, 113, 115–16, 118n, 119, 126, 132n
Sense and Non-Sense, xii, 46
Sheridan, J. F., 118n
Signs, 122, 126
Smart, B., 60
Socialisme ou Barbarie?, 112
Soviet Union, xii, 38–9, 45–7, 65, 69–70, 71–2, 87, 91, 94–6, 101, 118n, 119
Spiegelberg, H., 25
Stalin, J., 41n, 90, 94, 101, 108, 110–11, 118n
Structure of Behaviour, The, 4–7, 14, 18, 24

Telos, 60
Temps Modernes, Les, xi–xiii, 20, 38, 46, 97, 102–3, 118n, 119, 124–5
Textures, 130
Theses on Feuerbach, (Marx), 47–9
De Toqueville, A., 73
Tran-Duc-Thao, 60
Trotsky, L., 41n, 90, 105, 107–9, 127

Vietnam, xii, 89, 125
Visible and the Invisible, The, 120–1, 126, 128, 130, 131

De Waelhens, A., 112
Wahl, J., 4, 25
Weber, M., 103, 104, 123

LIBRARY OF DAVIDSON COLLEGE

...ks on regular loan ... out for **two weeks**. Books
... ...er to be renewed